MW01092177

IAMBLICHUS AND THE THEORY
OF THE VEHICLE OF THE SOUL

American Philological Association
American Classical Studies
Susan Treggiari, editor

John F. Finamore

Iamblichus and the Theory of the Vehicle of the Soul

Scholars Press
Chico, California

IAMBLICHUS AND THE THEORY
OF THE VEHICLE OF THE SOUL

John F. Finamore

© 1985
The American Philological Association

Library of Congress Cataloging in Publication Data

Finamore, John F., 1951–
    Iamblichus and the theory of the vehicle of the soul.

    (American classical studies ; no. 14)
    Bibliography: p.
    1. Iamblichus, ca. 250–ca. 330. 2. Soul—History of
doctrines—Early church, ca 30–600. I. Title. II. Series.
B669.Z7F55 1985   128'.1   85–10788
ISBN 0–89130–883–0 (alk. paper)

Printed in the United States of America
on acid-free paper

PARENTIBUS OPTIMIS

IOANNI ATQUE AMELIAE

SINE QUIBUS NON

TABLE OF CONTENTS

ACKNOWLEDGEMENTS

Thanks are owed to Antonia Tripolitis, Anna Benjamin, Robert
Bolton, and Michael Rohr, who formed my dissertation committee, and to
Roger Hornsby, who suggested several stylistic revisions. Early drafts
of several sections of this treatise were read at the American
Philological Association Meetings and at the University of Texas
at Austin. My work was improved by comments and questions of
classicists and philosophers attending those readings.

I wish to thank the reviewers of the American Philological
Association Monograph Board for their suggestions and corrections.
One of them, John M. Dillon, has made himself known to me. I owe
him a special debt of gratitude for his gracious and constructive
comments.

Finally, I owe special thanks to Susan McLean who, during
the time I have been researching, writing, and revising this work,
has helped me immensely both through discussions of neoplatonic
philosophy and through her unswerving moral support.

INTRODUCTION

The neoplatonic theory of the vehicle ὄχημα-πνεῦμα is,
as its ancient adherents perceived it, based upon the writings of
Plato and supported by those of Aristotle.[1] If one looks for such
supporting passages, however, one finds little with which to defend
the neoplatonists' claims. As Kissling (318) has said:

> The theory of the ὄχημα-πνεῦμα, as met with in the
> Neo-Platonic writers, represents the reconciliation of
> Plato and Aristotle on a subject which the former never
> taught and the latter was incapable of defining intel-
> ligibly.

How, then, do the neoplatonists conceive of the vehicle of the
soul, and with which Platonic and Aristotelian texts do they connect
that belief?

The vehicle is intended to join together two diametrically
opposed entities: the incorporeal soul and the corporeal body. It
is, therefore, neither material nor immaterial, but a mean between
these two extremes. Later philosophers claimed that ether, mentioned
in Epinomis 981c5-8 (a work they believed to be by Plato) and in
Aristotle's works (e.g., De Caelo 270b20-26), was the substance
comprising the vehicle.[2] For neoplatonists, the vehicle fulfills
three functions: it houses the rational soul in its descent from
the noetic realm to the realm of generation; it acts as the organ
of sense-perception and imagination; and, through theurgic rites, it
can be purified and lifted above, a vehicle for the rational soul's
return through the cosmos to the gods.

Neoplatonists were able to ascribe these functions to the
teachings of Plato and Aristotle. In Tim. 41e1-2, Plato says that
the Demiurge "distributed each [soul] to each [star], and having

1

mounted them [i.e., human souls] as if on a vehicle, he showed
them the nature of the universe." For a neoplatonist, the vehicle
is not the star but the ὄχημα-πνεῦμα. Once the soul is situated
on its own vehicle, it descends into generation. Neoplatonists
interpret, in a similar way, the myth of the Phaedrus, in which the
souls of the gods and humans are compared to charioteers riding in
chariots ὀχήματα, 247b1-3). For neoplatonists, each of these
passages shows a soul connected to its own vehicle both in the
cosmos and in the descent to earth.[3]

The vehicle's imaginative function depends upon Aristotelian
theory (e.g., De Gen. An. 744a1-5). Sense perceptions are impressed
upon the vehicle and can thereby be processed by the soul. (Note
that here again the vehicle is intermediary between the bodily
senses and the immaterial soul.) Furthermore, in De Gen. An. 736b37-
38, Aristotle says that the pneuma is "analogous to the element
comprising the stars" (ἀνάλογον οὖσα τῷ τῶν ἄστρων στοιχείῳ).
Thus, it is a simple step for later philosophers to combine Aristotle's
πνεῦμα with ether, the element of the stars, and with the "Platonic"
ὄχημα, onto which the Demiurge placed the soul.

From the doctrine of the soul's increasing materiality in
its descent,[4] the vehicle obtains its third, theurgic function. For
if the vehicle becomes stained by material additions in its descent,
purification from these material stains must be accomplished before
the soul can reascend. In accordance with religious practice of
the third and fourth centuries A.D., the purification of the vehicle
can occur in theurgic, ritual acts.

Plotinus attaches little importance to theurgy,[5] and, as a

3

result, is relatively unconcerned with the ὄχημα-πνεῦμα. He never
uses the term ὄχημα to refer to the soul's ethereal body. Nevertheless, Plotinus does seem to subscribe to a belief in an entity
like the vehicle.[6] In Enn. IV.3.15, in discussing the descent of
the soul, Plotinus says that when the soul leaves the noetic realm,
it goes "first into heaven and receives there a body through which
it continues into more earthy bodies" (lines 1-3). Here is the
notion, common in the later theories of the vehicle, of gradations
or envelopes of matter attaching themselves onto a primary body.
Plotinus seems to adopt the role of purification from these envelopes
at Enn. III.6.5.22-29:[7]

> But the purification of the part subject to affections
> is the waking up from inappropriate images and not seeing
> them, and its separation is effected by not inclining
> much downwards and not having a mental picture of the
> things below. But separating it could also mean taking away
> the things from which it is separated when it is not standing
> over a vital breath (πνεύματος) turbid from gluttony and
> sated with impure meats, but that in which it resides is so
> fine that it can ride on it (ἐπ᾽ αὐτοῦ ὀχεῖσθαι) in peace.

Here Plotinus clearly mentions the πνεῦμα in relation to its
purification and the soul's separation from the body. It would
seem that the soul can exist peacefully with its purified πνεῦμα
(although Plotinus is hesitant: εἴη δ᾽ ἄν, line 25). The use of
the verb ὀχεῖσθαι implies that Plotinus was familiar with the
term ὄχημα.[8]

In Enn. IV.3.24, Plotinus is again discussing the separation
of the soul from body (line 1: ἐξελθοῦσα τοῦ σώματος). In lines
20-28, where he is concerned with the punishment of souls in Hades,
Plotinus argues that souls with bodies receive bodily punishments
but those purified are in no way dragged (ἐφελκομέναις) by bodies

but exist entirely outside of them. As Smith (152) notes, the
participle ἐφελκομέναις is commonly used of the vehicle. Thus,
it would seem that, in harmony with the later neoplatonic interpretation of the Phaedo 113d4-6, Plotinus accepts the role of
πνεῦμα as substrate for souls punished in Hades.

No clear doctrine of the vehicle is seen to emerge from
Plotinus' writings.[9] It seems that if Plotinus knew of the writings
concerning the ὄχημα-πνεῦμα (and it is probable that he did), he
was not much interested in them.[10] It is with Porphyry and Iamblichus
that the doctrine becomes an integral part of neoplatonism.

As his treatise De Regressu Animae shows, Porphyry is concerned
to include the doctrine of the vehicle in his philosophical system.[11]
However, he allows theurgy power only over the vehicle itself. The
vehicle is purified by theurgy; the intellectual soul is separated
from the body not by theurgy but by philosophy (Fr. 2, pp. 28*, 2-29*,
1; Fr. 3, pp. 31*, 24-32*, 4; Fr. 4, p. 32*, 5-25; and Fr. 7, pp. 34*,
28-36*, 4). It is just this point that Iamblichus wishes to refute:
the only means of purification of the soul and its separation from
the body is through theurgy; philosophy alone is insufficient (De Myst.
II 11, pp. 96, 13-97, 11).

Emphasis on the importance of the role of the vehicle of
the soul is proportional to the importance one places on theurgy.
Plotinus, who cares little for such rites, is little concerned with
the vehicle. Porphyry, who is more interested in theurgy but still
considers such rites less valuable than philosophy, is more concerned
with the vehicle and has more to say about its role. Iamblichus
places the greatest importance on theurgy and, as a result, develops a

complete theory of the vehicle.

Unfortunately, not much has been written about Iamblichus'
conception of the role of the vehicle, and what little has been
written does not consider the importance of the vehicle to Iamblichus'
religious philosophy. The purpose of this study is to examine the
works of Iamblichus--especially the De Mysteriis, De Anima, and the
fragments of the Platonic commentaries--and to explain the role of
the soul's vehicle in Iamblichean philosophy. In section I, Iamblichus'
theory of the generation, composition, and ultimate fate of the vehicle
will be considered. It will be shown that Iamblichus' theory of the
vehicle is a reaction to Porphyry's. In sections II and III, two
studies will show the importance of the vehicle in Iamblichus' metaphysical system. It will be argued that Iamblichus creates a
hierarchical metaphysical system based upon his interpretation of
Plato's writings, especially of the Phaedrus and Timaeus. It will
also be shown how Iamblichus fits the vehicle, irrational soul, and
rational soul into this metaphysical hierarchy. Finally, in section IV,
the role of the vehicle in theurgy will be examined. The following
topics will be considered there: Iamblichus' conception of the
theurgic ritual's function in his religious philosophy, the role the
vehicle plays in this ritual, the ultimate fate of the vehicle, and
the religious reasons motivating Iamblichus to hold such an opinion
about the vehicle's fate.

One preliminary point should be raised. Iamblichus was the
author of many philosophical works over a period of approximately
forty-five years.[12] One should expect, therefore, that he would change
his mind occasionally and make later corrections to earlier theories.[13]

Nevertheless, with the exception of a very few problems mentioned below, Iamblichus' theory of the vehicle of the soul seems to be consistent over the course of his writings. This fact reinforces the view that Iamblichus is primarily a religious thinker. He might reconsider fine points, but he had made up his mind early about the important matter of the life of the vehicle of the soul.

Notes to Introduction

[1]There are several works on the neoplatonic theory of the
vehicle: R.C. Kissling, "The ὄχημα-πνεῦμα of the Neo-Platonists
and the De Insomniis of Synesius of Cyrene," AJP 43 (1922), 318-
330; E.R. Dodds, Proclus Elements of Theology, 2nd ed. (Oxford
1963), 315-321; J. Bidez, Vie de Porphyre (1913; rpt. Hildesheim
1964), 88-97; and A. Smith, Porphyry's Place in the Neoplatonic
Tradition (The Hague 1974), 152-158. These four studies deal
only slightly with Iamblichus. The following dwell more on
Iamblichus' opinion: G. Verbeke, L'Évolution de la Doctrine du
Pneuma du Stoïcisme à S. Augustin (Paris 1945), 374-384; J.M. Dillon,
Iamblichi Chalcidensis in Platonis Dialogos Commentariorum Fragmenta
(Leiden 1973), 47 and 371-377; and R.E. Witt, "Iamblichus as Fore-
runner of Julian," in De Jamblique à Proclus, ed. O. Reverdin
(Geneva 1975), 35-64. These works should be supplemented by E. des
Places, Jamblique Les Mystères d'Egypte (Paris 1966); A.J. Festugière's
translation (with notes) of Iamblichus' De Anima in Les Doctrines de
L'Ame, vol. III of La Révélation D'Hermès Trismégiste (Paris 1953),
177-248; and B.D. Larsen, Jamblique de Chalcis (Aarhus 1972), 2 vols.
For the vehicle of the soul in the Chaldaean Oracles, see H. Lewy,
Chaldaean Oracles and Theurgy, new edition edited by M. Tardieu
(Paris 1978), 178-184. The above works will be cited by the author's
name alone as will the following: A.D. Nock, Sallustius Concerning
the Gods and the Universe (Cambridge 1926); W. Scott, Hermetica,
vol. 4 (Oxford 1936); and R.T. Wallis, Neoplatonism (New York: 1972).
For the ancient texts cited below, see bibliography.

[2]The neoplatonists were not the first to do so. They
simply followed philosophic precedent. For earlier views, see
Dodds (316-318) and Dillon (371-372). For the neoplatonic combination of the Platonic passages dealing with the vehicle, see
especially Proclus, In Tim. III, pp. 234, 8-238, 26 and pp. 265,
15-268, 21.

[3]Cp. Plato, Phaedo 113d4-6: "Those who seemed to have lived
in a middle course [μεσῶς, i.e., neither exceptionally good nor
exceptionally bad] travel to Acheron, ascend onto their vehicles
(ἀναβάντες ἃ δὴ αὐτοῖς ὀχήματά ἐστιν), and arrive at the lake on
them." Neoplatonists interpreted this passage to mean that the
vehicle survived the human's death and remained with the human
soul in Hades.

[4]See Proclus, El. Th. prop. 209, and section I, below.

[5]See E.R. Dodds, The Greeks and the Irrational (Berkeley
1951), 285-286 and n. 25.

[6]On Plotinus' view of πνεῦμα see Dodds (318), Kissling
(322), Verbeke (352-363), and Smith (152-155).

[7]The translation is from A.H. Armstrong's edition of the
Enneads, III pp. 231-233. Note that Plotinus alludes to this
entity's imaginative function.

7

[8]But see Smith (153), who cites other uses of the verb by
Plotinus and argues that it is unsafe to place too much weight on
it here. However, since Dillon (371-372) has proven that a doctrine
of the ὄχημα-πνεῦμα existed in the second century A.D., it is
doubtful that Plotinus would have been unacquainted with it.

[9]Other passages cited by Smith (152-155) include Enn.
III.5.6.37, where Plotinus discusses the possibility of demons
possessing aery or fiery bodies (a conception probably based upon
Plato's Laws 898e10-899a2, as Dodds [315 and n. 3] suggests);
Enn. IV.3.9, where Plotinus distinguishes two methods by which the
soul enters the body: metempsychosis and "entering from an aery
or fiery body into an earthy one" (lines 5-6); and Enn. II.2.2.21,
where "the πνεῦμα around the soul" is said to move in a circle,
but this passage probably refers to Tim. 79a5-e9 and its discussion
of respiration, as both Smith (153) and Armstrong, in his edition
of the Enneads, II, p. 46 n. 2, believe.

[10]The troublesome beginning of Enn. I.9.1.1 (concerning
suicide) cannot be discussed at length here. According to Psellus,
Exposition 1125d1-1126b7, Plotinus' opening words (οὐκ ἐξάξεις,
ἵνα μὴ ἐξίῃ ἐξελεύσεται γὰρ ἔχουσά τι) derive from the Chaldaean
Oracles (=Fr. 166): μὴ 'ξάξῃς, ἵνα μὴ τι ἔχουσα ἐξίῃ. Lewy
(474) argues that Psellus has misread his source (i.e., Proclus), who
probably attributed the Oracle to the Orphics. Dodds (note 5,
above) 285 and 301-302 n. 26 believes that Plotinus' words are
Pythagorean and that Plotinus knew nothing of the Chaldaean Oracles.
Armstrong, in his edition of the Enneads, I, pp. 322-323 n. 1, is
unsure "whether Plotinus is quoting the oracle or whether the oracle
was later taken from Plotinus." In response, des Places, in his
edition of the Chaldaean Oracles, p. 165 n. 1, points out that the
Oracles had been written long before Plotinus wrote, but he admits
that the words in Psellus' Oracle do not fit well into the hexameter
meter of the other Oracles. Smith (154) conceded only that
Plotinus "would appear to be quoting the Chaldaean Oracles . . .
and they certainly believed in the ὄχημα-πνεῦμα." In defense of
a Chaldaean source for Plotinus' words, it should be said (1) that
there is no other parallel case of Psellus misquoting from Proclus'
lost commentary on the Chaldaean Oracles (Psellus' addition to Fr.
164 is a different matter entirely); (2) that there is nothing in
the Oracle with which Plotinus would disagree, so that even if
there were much in the Oracles that he would find disconcerting,
Plotinus would not object to quoting this doctrine; and (3) Plotinus
most probably would have come into contact with Chaldaean beliefs
from his students, as, for example, is the case with certain gnostic
writings (see vit. Plot. 16).

[11]On the role of the vehicle in Porphyry's writings, see
Dodds (318-319), Kissling (322-323, 324-325), Verbeke (363-373),
Smith (155-158), and Bidez (88-97). Porphyry believes that the
vehicle is the seat of imagination (De Regr. Fr. 2, p. 28*, 5-6),
that it survives for the soul's punishment in Hades (Sent. 29),
and that the vehicle becomes increasingly material during its

descent into the realm of generation (apud Proclus, In Tim.
III, p. 234, 18-32). The fragments of Porphyry's De Regressu
have been collected by Bidez (Appendix II, pp. 27*-44*).

[12]For a list of Iamblichus' writings and an attempt to place
them in chronological order, see Dillon (18-25). As Dillon himself
notes (18), his attempt is "provisional."

[13]See especially Proclus, In Tim. I, pp. 307, 14-309, 13,
where Proclus compares what Iamblichus says about the Demiurge in
his Timaeus commentary (Fr. 34) with his treatise, "On the Speech
of Zeus in the Timaeus." On this treatise, see Dillon (417-419),
307-309).

[14]Although I do believe that the theory was worked out in
greater detail in the Platonic commentaries than in the De Mysteriis
or De Anima.

I. Iamblichus and Porphyry on the Vehicle's
Composition, Generation, and Fate

Iamblichus' conception of the vehicle was directed against
Porphyry's. He disagreed with Porphyry on three separate points: the
composition, generation, and ultimate fate of the vehicle.

Iamblichus dismissed Porphyry's claim that the vehicle was
composed of a series of mixtures (φυράματα) collected from the
celestial spheres.[1] In his <u>Timaeus</u> commentary, Iamblichus asserts
that the vehicle was made of παντὸς τοῦ αἰθέρος (i.e., from ether
itself, not from several ethereal bodies) and that this ether had a
creative power.

The composition of the vehicle was closely linked to its
generation. In <u>In Tim</u>. Fr. 81, Iamblichus states that the vehicle did
not simply derive its existence from the celestial bodies (otherwise
the vehicle would be changeable by its very nature: μεταβλητόν . . .
κατὰ τὴν ἑαυτοῦ φύσιν[2]) and that its origin was "from the gods
themselves, who organize the Cosmos and perform all their acts
eternally."[3] Furthermore, in <u>In Tim</u>. Fr. 84, Iamblichus adds that the
generation of the vehicle is brought about without any loss of
substance to the celestial gods and without having been collected from
them (οὔτε ἐλαττουμένων τῶν θείων σωμάτων οὔτε συμπεφορημένως τούτων
ὑφισταμένων.)[4] What Iamblichus is concerned to show is made clear
from what follows this fragment in Proclus.[5] The Demiurge himself
produces the vehicle. The vehicle is, therefore, "somehow self-
constituted and not created by subtraction (ἀφαίρεσις) from others in
order that it not require dissolution (ἀνάχυσις) back into another"
(Proclus, <u>In Tim</u>. III, p. 267, 20-22).

11

For Iamblichus, then, the Demiurge creates the vehicle whole.
Does this mean that Iamblichus totally rejects the belief that the
soul accumulated vestments in its descent through the cosmos? There
are indications of an answer that points to a typically Iamblichean
separation of gods from human beings.

Nowhere in Iamblichus' writings does he explicitly accept a
doctrine of vestments. That he is aware of the term περιβλήματα is
apparent from De An. I, p. 385, 6-7. Nevertheless, Iamblichus does
not say that he accepts these ethereal, heavenly, and pneumatic
envelopes. Stobaeus' extract from the De Anima ends abruptly (at p.
385, 10) before Iamblichus gives his own opinion.[6]

In De Myst. II 5, p. 4-14, Iamblichus says that ἀτμοὶ
περικόσμιοι mix with demons, γενεσιουργοὶ πνευμάτων συντάσεις with
heroes, and that souls are filled with περισσῶν μολυσμῶν καὶ ἀλλοτρίων
πνευμάτων. Moreover, in De Myst. II 7, p. 84, 14-18, unpurified souls
are laden with accumulations (συστάσεις) of hylic πνεύματα, held down
by ταραχαὶ ὕλης ἀνώμαλοι, and seen with genesiourgic demons. There
is, however, no suggestion that these πνεύματα come from the celestial
gods. Indeed, in De Myst. V 4, pp. 201, 12-205, 14, Iamblichus seems
to deny that they do. The whole thrust of this latter chapter
suggests that the celestial gods are separate from them.

This is not to say that Iamblichus rejected any interaction
between the celestial gods and the vehicle. In In Tim. Fr. 84, he
states that the origin of the vehicle was "not simply" (ουχ ἁπλῶς)
from the celestial gods. This suggests that they have some connection
to the vehicle. Iamblichus goes on to explain their role: the
vehicles proceeded from and were shaped by ζωαὶ θεῖαι. As Dillon

(380) explains, these are the "unreasoning generative principles . . .
of the encosmic gods." Given, however, the absolute goodness of the
encosmic gods (see, for example, De Myst. I 18, p. 53, 2-5),[7] these
ζωαί were doubtless beneficial and, thus, not the πνεύματα of De Myst
II 5 and 7.

These ζωαί are mentioned again in a quotation from Iamblichus
in Simplicius' commentary on Aristotle's Categories.[8] The passage
concerns the Aristotelian category of "having" (ἔχειν). In this
passage, Iamblichus differentiates between what the soul has from
itself and what it receives from the outside. The soul has certain
acquired lives (ἐπίκτητοί τινες ζωαί), some of which are of a similar
nature (ὁμοφυείς) to the soul and others inferior to the appropriate
measures of the soul. The soul also projects (προβάλλει)[9] lives
around itself and accepts (παραδέχεται) others from the physical body
itself. Iamblichus continues:

> When the soul comes into each part of the cosmos, it accepts
> certain lives and powers (δυνάμεις), some of which it
> projects itself and others it receives (λαμβάνουσα) from the
> cosmos. In each part of the universe, there are appropriate
> bodies (σώματα), some it receives from the cosmos and other
> organic bodies it makes in accordance with its own λόγοι.
> These powers, lives, and bodies it puts aside (ἀποτίθεται)
> whenever it changes to another allotment (λῆξις). From this,
> it is clear that all these are acquired for the soul and that
> the soul has them as different from its own essence.

This passage discusses the soul's descent from the heavens
into the physical body. In its descent, the soul accumulates various
lives, powers, and (lastly) organic bodies. What are the roles of
these added entities?

According to In Tim. Fr. 84, the pneumatic vehicle is given
shape (μορφούμενον) by the divine lives. In Tim. Fr. 49 states that

the vehicle is spherical, a shape most proper to the soul's self-movement and intellection. Did the Demiurge create the vehicle and leave it to the cosmic gods to form it into a sphere? This seems absurd. Rather, it seems that these ζωαί re-shape the spherical vehicle.[10] The kind of shaping that is done is not explained. It seems most probable, however, that the divine lives enter the vehicle and promote the rational activities of the soul. (These would be the acquired lives that are of a similar nature to the soul.) Other lives, such as those that the Simplicius passage terms "inferior to the appropriate measures of the soul," would be irrational and would distort the normal rational activity of the pure soul.[11]

There are, then, two different stages in the soul's life. First, there is the rational soul itself existing by itself. Second, there is the rational soul in a body. Iamblichus elsewhere refers to this as the double life.[12] Only the innate lives and powers belong to the rational soul. It is to the composite life of soul and body that the irrational and rational powers and lives attach themselves. Since this is the case, all the lives, powers, and bodies that the soul accumulates in the descent are acquired by and not innate to the rational soul. Thus, when Iamblichus says (De An. I, pp. 367, 22-368, 6) that the powers are present in one way to the rational soul and in another to the composite of soul and body, he means that they are essentially connected to the rational soul, but only acquired by the composite. As Iamblichus says in the Simplicius passage, the lives, powers, and bodies are separate from the soul's essence.[13]

It is also worth noting that the "common life" itself involves two parts: the vehicle and the corporeal body.[14] Thus, while the vehicle receives lives and powers from different places in the cosmos, it is clear that it can receive corporeal bodies only in the sublunar region where matter exists. The soul, therefore, becomes more and more material in its descent. In this respect, Iamblichus' conception is similar to the one that Proclus gives in El. Th. Prop. 209. According to Proclus, the vehicle descends and gathers χιτῶνες that become more and more material the lower it descends. Proclus says that the soul "descends receiving irrational ζωάς and ascends removing all its γενεσιουργοὺς δυνάμεις, which it put around itself in its descent" (p. 182, 19-21). Iamblichus also believed that the powers, lives, and bodies would be set aside in the soul's ascent to a higher λῆξις.

Iamblichus' theory on the vestments gathered during the soul's descent can now be understood. He is making a great departure from his predecessors' beliefs. In De An. I, p. 385, 5-10, he describes a group of philosophers who held that the ethereal, heavenly, and pneumatic envelopes were attached to the rational soul (νοερὰ ζωή) and served it as vehicles. Iamblichus would argue that these envelopes are not the vehicle but, rather, are the lives, powers, and bodies attached to the ethereal vehicle itself. Thus, for Iamblichus, the vehicle itself is ethereal, it picks up its heavenly "envelopes" from the lives and powers in the universe, and finally it attracts certain "foreign πνεύματα" from the sublunar region.

The last of the three points of disagreement between Iamblichus and Porphyry concerned the vehicle's ultimate fate. Iamblichus, according to In Tim. Fr. 81, believed that both the

vehicle and the irrational soul were immortal. Some passages from his
De Anima help to clarify what is at issue.[15]

In De An. I, p. 370, 5-13, Iamblichus claims that "those
around Plotinus and Porphyry" say that certain irrational powers
(δυνάμεις) are projected (προβάλλεσθαι) in each part of the universe.
They also claim that the lives (ζωαί) thus projected "are released and
no longer exist." Iamblichus himself[16] believes that "even these
exist in the universe and are not destroyed."

The mention of δυνάμεις and ζωαί is reminiscent of the
Simplicius passage referred to above. That passage was concerned with
the addition of δυνάμεις and ζωαί during the soul's descent through
the cosmos. The passage in the De Anima is concerned with the
shedding of them during the soul's reascent. In the Simplicius
passage,, Iamblichus claimed that the soul puts them aside (ἀποτίθεται)
whenever it changes to another allotment. In the De Anima, it is seen
that both Porphyry and Iamblichus agree that the irrational powers and
lives are released from the soul, but Porphyry thinks that they cease
to exist whereas Iamblichus claims that they continue to exist in the
universe.

More light is shed on this issue in De An. I, p. 384, 19-28.
Here it is said that "those around Plotinus" separated the irrational
powers from the rational part (λόγος). These philosophers believe
either that the irrational powers are released into generation or that
they are taken away from the faculty of discursive thought (διάνοια).
This latter view can be interpreted in two ways. The first
interpretation, Iamblichus says, is Porphyry's: "each irrational
power (δύναμις) is freed into the whole life of the universe from

which it was parted, where[17] as much as possible each remains

unchanged (ἀμετάβλητος)." The second is Iamblichus':[18] "the whole

irrational life, having been separated from the διάνοια remains and is

itself preserved in the cosmos."

Both Festugière (236 n. 2) and Smith (64-66) have noted the

seeming inconsistency in Porphyry's position as given by Iamblichus in

these two passages. These modern authors cite Proclus' Timaeus

commentary (III, p. 234, 18-26) as an aid to understanding Porphyry's

beliefs.[19] Proclus places Porphyry directly between those who say

that the vehicle and irrational soul are mortal (viz., Atticus and

Albinus, p. 234, 9-18) and those who say they are immortal (viz.,

Iamblichus). Porphyry, according to Proclus, denied that the vehicle

and irrational soul were destroyed but claimed that they were

> broken into their elements (ἀναστοιχειοῦσθαι) and dissolved
> in some way into the spheres from which they obtained their
> composition, and that these mixtures (φυράματα) are from the
> heavenly spheres and the soul collects them during its
> descent so that they [i.e., the mixtures] both exist and do
> not exist, and that each of these separately (ἕκαστα) no
> longer exists nor does their individuality (ἰδιότητα) remain.

For Porphyry, the vehicle and irrational soul were made up of

bits of the heavenly spheres and their ultimate fate was to return to

the cosmos. The mixtures are dissolved but still exist separately

from the soul.

Iamblichus' view is more complex. In response to Porphyry,

Iamblichus stated (In Tim. Fr. 81) that the vehicle and irrational

soul are immortal. Further, since the vehicle is not made up of

mixtures but is created whole (In Tim. Fr. 84), it will continue to

live on as a whole after its separation from the soul. The immortal

irrational soul and the immortal vehicle in which it is housed receive various lives and powers from the cosmos. When the soul ascends to a higher λῆξις, these lives and powers are put aside. The change in λῆξις is the change from the cosmic, embodied soul to the hypercosmic, disembodied soul. The "putting off," therefore, is the separation of the rational soul from its vehicle and irrational soul. The various lives and powers are not released into the universe so that they are separate and, in a certain sense, non-existent (i.e., cease to exist as a single entity). Rather, they are separated from the rational soul but subsist within the vehicle and irrational soul, which themselves continue to exist in the cosmos.

This is Iamblichus' "newer thought" (De An. I, p. 370, 13). The lives and powers are released but not dispersed. This is also the teaching of the priests (De An. I, p. 384, 26-27). Where Porphyry went wrong, in Iamblichus' opinion, was in thinking that each power (ἑκάστη, line 23; ἕκαστα in the Proclus passage above) returned separately to the cosmos. For Iamblichus, the whole irrational life (ὅλη ἄλογος ζωή, line 26) remains and is preserved (as a complete entity) in the cosmos.

There is another point worth noting here. Porphyry had argued that the irrational soul was dissolved yet remained ὅτι μάλιστα . . . ἀμετάβλητος (De An. I, p. 384, 24-25). Iamblichus seems to have had this curious phrase in mind when he argued that the vehicle would be changeable (μεταβλητόν) in its own nature if it were created only from divine bodies (In Tim. Fr. 81). In other words, Iamblichus was saying that the vehicle (and the irrational soul and powers in it) can remain ἀμετάβλητον only if the vehicle is created by unmoving causes.[20]

After citing these three passages from the De Anima and from
Proclus, Smith (67) sums up the difference between Porphyry's and
Iamblichus' views as follows. The difference can

> be traced precisely to the mode in which the irrational soul
> lives on. For Iamblichus the whole irrational soul lives on
> whilst for Porphyry there is some kind of dissolution of the
> component powers which somehow continue to exist in a
> separated state. Clearly the integral irrational personality
> as vested in the irrational soul has greater significance in
> Iamblichus.

The question that arises is why should Iamblichus stress the
immortality of the vehicle and the irrational soul? Proclus (In Tim.
III, p. 235, 11-27) suggests one possibility: that the vehicle must
survive the body in order for souls to use them in Hades (Phaedo
113d). There is, however, another possibility.

In a badly marred chapter of his De Anima (I, pp. 457, 7-458,
21)[21] Iamblichus discusses the soul's reward (ἐπικαρπία). Throughout
this chapter, Iamblichus is dealing with the soul's departure from the
body (ἐπειδὰν ἐξέλθωσι τοῦ σώματος, p. 457, 9) and the separation of
the rational soul from the vehicle. Twice in this account, Iamblichus
touches upon Porphyry's beliefs about the irrational soul. Although
both passages are marred by lacunae, they help to explain why
Iamblichus thought that the vehicle was immortal.

The first passage appears in a section concerning what
belongs to the rational soul itself (p. 457, 13-22). This passage is
divided into two comparisons between the ancients (ἀρχαιότεροι, line
13, and πρεσβυτέρων τινές, lines 16-17) and Porphyry. The ancients
here, as in p. 384, 27-28, represent Iamblichus' opinion.[22] In the
first comparison, the ancients say that the rational soul has "a
disposition similar to the gods in intellect and a charge (προστασία)

over things here [i.e., in the realm of generation]." In contrast,
Porphyry does not allow that disembodied souls have such authority
over the encosmic realm.[23]

The second comparison between the ancients and Porphyry is as
follows.

> Some of the ancients say that it [i.e., the rational soul]
> excels the reasoning element (λογισμός) and they define its
> [i.e., the rational soul's] acts (ἔργα) so carefully that not
> even the pure and most perfect reasoning elements could
> attain them . . . Porphyry removes them (αὐτάς) altogether
> from the independent life (ἀδέσποτος ζωή), as being naturally
> attached to generation and given as an aid to composite
> beings (σύνθετα ζῷα).

Festugière (245 n. 1) has noted the lacuna (marked above by
an ellipsis) in this passage. He has correctly argued that the word
αὐτάς (line 20) cannot refer to souls since Porphyry could not have
argued that the souls are separated from the independent life (i.e.,
the life of the soul separated from body). Festugière therefore
assumes that αὐτάς refers to the irrational powers. He then suggests
the following reading for the lacuna: "The ancients (sc. Iamblichus)
have declared that the inferior δυνάμεις (or ἐνέργειαι) of the soul
are immortal."

Festugière is certainly right about the referent of αὐτάς.
As he himself points out, the previous lines mention the reasoning
element and it is only natural to speak next of the irrational
element. If this interpretation is correct, Porphyry's position here
is the same as it was before: the irrational powers do not belong to
the disembodied soul and, therefore, are separated from it.

The problem with Festugière's reading is not the
interpretation of αὐτάς, but the extent of the lacuna. As Festugière

himself points out (245 n. 1) Iamblichus' entire chapter is based upon antitheses. The first passage (p. 457, 13-22) was based upon an antithesis between the opinions of the ancients and those of Porphyry. One would expect, then, a Porphyrian stance corresponding to that of the ancients concerning the separation of the rational element from the disembodied soul.

The problem here is deciding what Iamblichus thought was separated. A comparison of the present passage with De An. I, p. 384, 19-28 shows that there are three faculties of the soul dealt with here. First, the irrational life is separated from the διάνοια (p. 384, 26); second, the rational soul has an "ἀγαθοειδῆ disposition similar to the gods κατὰ νοῦν" (p. 457, 14); and finally, the rational soul excels the λογισμός (p. 457, 17). The reader is left to infer that the λογισμός is a lower rational faculty that is shed during the soul's reascent.[24] The διάνοια, on the other hand, is a higher rational faculty. It and the intellectual disposition comprise the disembodied soul.[25] The lacuna in the present passage, therefore, should have included a reference to Porphyry's view on the relation of soul to intellect (or, more precisely, to the intellectual disposition in the soul).

Iamblichus had mentioned Porphyry's beliefs on the relationship between soul and higher entities in two earlier passages in the De Anima (p. 365, 17-19 and p. 372, 12-14)[26]. In the first of these two passages, Iamblichus is contrasting two possible points of view concerning the soul's relation to the entities above it. After stating that Numenius, Plotinus, and Amelius believe that the soul is the same as intellect and the other higher entities, Iamblichus turns to Porphyry's opinion on this identification of soul and intellect. Porphyry, he says, "is in doubt about this [identification]; sometimes he earnestly rejects it, sometimes he accepts it." In the second passage, Iamblichus discusses whether all souls accomplish the same acts (ἔργα) or different acts according to the soul's rank. Here he opposes Porphyry to the Stoics, Plotinus, and Amelius with regard to the acts of the Universal and particular souls: "As Porphyry would say, the operations (ἐνεργήματα) of the Universal Soul are entirely separated from the particular soul."

Iamblichus' own opinion in these two passages is that the soul is separated from intellect "in another hypostasis" (p. 365, 24) and that its acts differed from the acts of other, higher souls.[27] For Iamblichus, the rational soul is not intellect but has an intellectual disposition, Thus, he can keep soul and intellect separate.

It is difficult to determine what Iamblichus would have given as Porphyry's opinion in the lacuna (p. 457, 19). As can be seen, Iamblichus was hesitant about Porphyry's exact opinion at p. 365, 17-19. Despite this hesitancy, however, Iamblichus proceeds to rank Porphyry together with Amelius and Plotinus as believing that the soul does not differ from the intellect (p. 365, 19-21). At p. 372, 12-14, it is clear that Porphyry's separation of the acts of the Universal Soul from those of particular souls was not sufficient for Iamblichus' purpose[28] since Iamblichus goes on to introduce his own opinion as differing from Porphyry's (ἄλλη δόξα, p. 372, 15). This evidence suggests that Iamblichus ranked Porphyry with the other Platonists on these issues.

This is Festugière's opinion as well (199 n. 1). He includes Porphyry among the Platonists mentioned in another passage concerning the relationship between the soul and intellect (De An. I, p. 318, 12-15):

> Many of the Platonists themselves introduce the intellect into the soul at the same time as the first entry of soul into body, and they do not differentiate at all between the soul and its intellect.

Another passage (p. 457, 11-12), however, creates serious problems for anyone holding the opinion that Iamblichus ranked Porphyry together with these other Platonists.[29] Here Iamblichus says that Porphyry "keeps the soul in its proper order (τάξις)." Thus, only a few lines before the lacuna, Iamblichus states that Porphyry did keep soul and intellect separate.

Iamblichus' disagreement with Porphyry is, it seems, more subtle. As has been seen, Iamblichus granted that Porphyry separated the ἐνεργήματα of the Universal and particular souls (p. 372, 12-14). This separation, although closer to Iamblichus' view than Plotinus' or Amelius' was, did not satisfy Iamblichus. He goes on to give his own view[30] that not only do the acts of the Universal and particular souls differ, but so do those of divine, demonic, heroic, and human souls (p. 372, 15-20). Furthermore, Iamblichus adds (p. 373, 3-8):[31]

> The ἐνεργήματα of Universal, divine, and immaterial souls end in essence, but those of particular souls, which souls are held in one form and divided around bodies, are by no means . . . immediately the same as that which they accomplish.

Dillon (44) describes the distinction as follows:

> Divine souls, for instance, perform acts which do not end in any accomplishment distinct from their essence . . . whereas in the case of human souls, their acts extend outwards and are not identical with their essence.

At p. 457, 16-19, Iamblichus is discussing the different acts not of different souls, but of different phases within the same soul: the acts of the disembodied soul differ from those of the λογισμός. For Iamblichus, the disembodied soul sheds its lower powers and lives and enters a higher allotment. The disembodied soul is completely immaterial and disassociated from all bodies, including the ethereal vehicle. As such, its acts become more like those of divine souls; that is, its acts tend to end in essence.

If this explanation is correct, Iamblichus' complaint against Porphyry remains much the same as before. It is not a matter of Porphyry confusing soul and intellect, but a matter of Porphyry confusing (or not separating precisely enough for Iamblichus' tastes) the acts of embodied and disembodied soul.

In the original passage (p. 457, 13-22), then, there is now a triple, instead of double, comparison:

(1) The ancients attribute to the soul both an intellectual disposition and an authority over things in the encosmic realm; Porphyry removes this authority

(2) The ancients separate the λογισμός from the disembodied soul and define the acts of each differently; Porphyry does not adequately differentiate their acts

(3) The ancients say that the inferior powers of the soul are immortal; Porphyry removes them from the disembodied soul.

These points of disagreement are given in descending order. In other words, reading from (3) to (1), Iamblichus recounts the soul's ascent to its reward. A soul casts off its irrational powers and lower rational powers, acts in accordance with its intellectual disposition, and gains as part of its reward an authority over this realm.

An important passage from the De Mysteriis (V 18, pp. 223, 9-224, 1) helps to clarify the issue. Here Iamblichus is discussing a difference between the great herd (ἀγέλη) of human beings, who are under nature and fate, and a certain few who are separated from nature. The first group always uses πρακτικὸς λογισμός (p. 223, 14) about single entities in nature. The second group is described as follows (pp. 223, 15-224, 1):

> A certain few, using some supernatural power of intellect, stand apart from nature, and are led around to the separated and unmixed intellect, and become superior to physical powers.

The division of human beings resembles the distinction between the human soul that has its reasoning element and the disembodied human soul with its intellectual disposition. The passage from the De Mysteriis suggests that the reward, which the De Anima attributes to disembodied souls, is achieved by only a few souls. Such a disembodied soul is led to another allotment, to the Intellect. This is the reward for theurgists.[32] They become superior to nature and have authority over it.

The second passage in the De Anima (p. 458, 12-17) also mentions the soul's authority. In this passage, "those around Porphyry" are compared with "the Platonists." The passage is marred by lacunae, but the meaning is clear. Iamblichus is discussing the extent of the soul's reward. [33]

> Those around Porphyry <say that the reward (or: immortality) is extended> to human lives. But they posit another form (εἶδος) of soul after this, the irrational. Moreover, Porphyry makes the soul similar to the Universe, while the soul remains in itself what it is <but he does not think that it presides over things here.> According to the Platonists, souls have charge of inanimate entities (ἄψυχα).

As in De An. I, p. 457, 13-22, there is a distinction between the rational (ἀνθρώπινοι βίοι)[34] and irrational (ἀλόγιστοι) lives coupled with the concept of the soul's authority over this realm (ἐπιμελοῦνται). For Iamblichus (as opposed to Porphyry), the separation of the rational soul from the irrational soul is somehow connected to this concept.

There is, then, another disagreement that helps to explain one reason for Iamblichus' belief that the vehicle and irrational soul are immortal. Porphyry believed that the philosopher's soul escaped from the cosmic realm permanently.[35] Thus, he denied any further encosmic role to such souls, including exercising authority over inanimate entities in it. Iamblichus, on the other hand, believed that even a soul that ascended into the noetic realm had to return to this realm, although such a soul does make a descent that is unconnected with generation and without a break with the noetic (In Phaed. Fr. 5).[36] Since in this latter case the soul descends again to the earth, the fragment shows that Iamblichus believed that all souls must return to this cosmos.

In the De Anima, however, Iamblichus is concerned with the soul's reward after death. For Iamblichus, this reward includes a return to this realm and an authority over things in it. De An. I, p. 458, 17-21 explains this reward. According to the ancients (παλαιοί), souls "are freed from generation and together with the gods administer (συνδιοικοῦσι) the universe."[37] Moreover, "along with the angels, they oversee (συνδημιουργοῦσι) the universe."

It is clear that since Porphyry denied any further association with this realm for those philosophers escaping it, the immortality of the vehicle was not an issue. The philosopher's soul would not need the vehicle again. For Iamblichus, however, the soul of the theurgist must return to his purified vehicle and, therefore, the the vehicle must remain intact.[38] The religious reasons for Iamblichus' belief will be examined in section IV below.

Porphyry's and Iamblichus' differences concerning the vehicle can be summed up as follows: for Porphyry the vehicle is created from portions of the bodies of the visible gods and perishes when these portions are sloughed off, whereas for Iamblichus it is ethereal and created whole by the Demiurge, and not subject to destruction or dissolution of any kind.

[1]Proclus, In Tim. III, p. 234, 18-26 (translated below, p. 16), cited by Dillon (372-373), Dodds (319), Verbeke (365), Kissling (322, 324-325), Smith (66), and Festugière (127).

[2]Compare De An. ap. Stobaeus I, p. 374, 2, where Iamblichus calls vehicles αὐτοειδέσι πνεύμασι. Festugière (206) translates: "certain pneumatic bodies of a nature always identical to itself." See also his notes 4 and 5 ad loc.

[3]The translation is Dillon's (195).

[4]See Dillon (380), though he now rejects his original translation of συμπεφορημένως.

[5]Proclus, In Tim. III, pp. 266, 31-267, 11. Since Iamblichus believes that the vehicle did not originate in moving causes (In Tim. Fr. 81), the vehicle's cause must be unmoved. This points to the Demiurge. Note that Proclus agrees that the vehicle is created by an unmoved cause (El. Th. prop. 207 and Dodd's note, p. 306). Note also that what Proclus says a little further on (In Tim. III, p. 268, 10-18) is Iamblichean doctrine (e.g., De An. I, p. 379, 12-15 and De Myst. I 17, p. 50, 16-51, 9). Proclus appears to be interweaving Iamblichean ideas throughout this discussion.

[6]According to Festugière (237 n. 4), the doctrine of the περιβλήματα is "present in Hermetic or Christian gnosis," and he notes the similarity between a passage from the Corpus Hermeticum and Iamblichus' words. Iamblichus would have continued after p. 385, 10 much as he did in 384, 19-28; that is, he would go on to give the views of Plotinus, Porphyry, and the priests. For a review of the concept of vestments (χιτῶνες), see Dodds (307-308).

[7]See also Larsen (181).

[8]Simplicius, in Arist. Categ. p. 374 ff. Kalbfleisch. A translation is given by Festugière (196 n. 2).

[9]For the meaning of the verb προβάλλειν, "to project from itself," see especially De Myst. II 2, p. 68, 12-13: the soul projecting (προβάλλουσα) different forms (εἴδη), reasons (λόγους), and lives (βίους). Cp. Iamblichus' De Communi Mathematica Scientia, p. 44, 7-10, where Iamblichus says that the soul is reminded of the true forms in mathematics and then brings forth from itself (προβάλλει) the λόγοι appropriate to them. See also p. 43, 21, where the ἔργον of the mathematical science calls forth from itself (ἀφ' ἑαυτοῦ προβάλλει) the principle of recollection.

[10]Dillon (380) thinks that these ζοαί are "in theological terms, the aetherial source of the individual πνεύματα/ὀχήματα This cannot be the case. If the ζοαί were a source of ether, then

the vehicles would accumulate bits of ether in its descent. But this is exactly what Iamblichus denies. For ζωαί in Porphyry, see Smith (3).

[11]Another source of these ζωαί is the sublunar demiurge. In In Sophistam Fr. 1, Iamblichus says that the sublunar demiurge "projects from himself many essences and lives (οὐσίας καὶ ζωὰς προβεβλημένος) through which he establishes the diversity of generation." These οὐσίαι and ζωαί are, of course, sublunar and hylic. (Note that this demiurge "charms souls with physical λόγοι.") See also In Tim. Fr. 75 where the goddess Ge, understood in Tim. 40e5 as what is permanent and fixed in the encosmic gods, embraces the greater powers and whole lives (δυνάμεις κρείττονας καὶ ζωὰς ὅλας). These are not hylic. Cf. De Myst. I 18.

[12]De Myst. III 3, p. 106, 3-4; De An. I, p. 368, 3-6; p. 370, 3-4; p. 371, 4-6. See Festugière (192 n. 2, 195 n. 4, and 200 n. 7) and des Places (101 n. 2). For the double life in Porphyry's philosophy, see Stob. I, p. 345, 11-12 and Smith (3).

[13]See De An. I, p. 371, 6-7, where the ἐνεργήματα of the soul itself differ from those of the composite. The powers of the soul are listed on p. 369, 13-15, and later (p. 370, 3-4) Iamblichus says that Plato ascribes the powers to the soul itself and to the composite life, distinguishing each in accordance with each life. Cf., Festugière (195 n. 4 and 199 n. 2).

[14]This is also apparent from De Myst. III 3, p. 106, 4, where the life of the rational soul is said to be separate from every body (παντὸς σώματος), i.e., both ethereal and corporeal bodies.

[15]See Smith (64-67) who believes that both Iamblichus and Proclus misconstrued Porphyry's view about the vehicle. (But see note 38 below.) Smith cites De An. I, p. 370 and p. 384.

[16]The words "perhaps someone might think not unpersuasively a newer thought" (p. 370, 12-13) express Iamblichus' own opinion. See Festugière (196 n. 1 and 189 n. 3) and Larsen (206).

[17]For this reading, see Dillon (375-376) and Smith (65 n. 19).

[18]Here the "most ancient of priests" (lines 26-27) represent Iamblichus' opinion. See Festugière (262-264), Dillon (375), Smith (65), and Larsen (206 n. 27).

[19]The passage, which immediately precedes In Tim. Fr. 81, is discussed by Dillon (372-373).

[20]A similar argument is made by Proclus (El. Th. prop. 208, p. 182, 12-15). The vehicle is indivisible because it is unchangeable (ἀμετάβλητον line 14).

[21]See Festugière (245 n. 1) for the various textual problems.

[22]See Festugière (245 n. 1): "Les anciens (sc. Jamblique). . ."

[23]Reading τοῦτο (p. 457, 16) with Heeren, Wachsmuth, and Festugière (246 n. 6). The manuscripts read τούτους, which is impossible.

[24]Plotinus had already said that disembodied souls do not use λογισμός. See Festugière (247 n. 1), where he cites Plotinus IV 3, 18. The λογισμός, for Iamblichus, probably represents the lives ὁμοφυεῖς to the soul, mentioned in the Simplicius passage above. It, like the irrational lives and powers, is acquired in the soul's descent and laid aside when the soul ascends to a higher allotment. Porphyry seems to separate the λογισμός from the soul's higher functions in Sent. 32, where he talks about the different kinds of virtues. Political virtue is associated with "following and being guided by λογισμός" (p. 23, 4-6, cf. lines 8-12). Λογισμός is involved with πάθος (p. 25, 2-3; cf. p. 34, 10-14).

[25]Iamblichus follows Plato (Rep. 511d4-5, where διάνοια is ranked between δόξα and νοῦς cf. ib. d8-e4, where it is placed between νόησις on the one hand, and πίστις and εἰκασία on the other) in ranking διάνοια between opinion (δόξα), on the one side, and intellect (νοῦς ὁ ψυχικός) and intellection (νόησις μετὰ λόγου), on the other (In Parm. Fr. 2A). See also Proclus, El. Th. prop. 123, pp. 108, 32-110, 3, where διάνοια is also ranked between δόξα and νόησις. Dodds, in his note to this passage (265), compares Proclus, In Parm. p. 1081, 7-11. Since, for Iamblichus, the soul is "the mean between partial and impartial and corporeal and incorporeal kinds" (De An. I, pp. 365, 28-366, 1; see also, the passages translated by Festugière in his Note Complémentaire III, p. 252-257), it seems most appropriate that the soul should include the διάνοια which also operates as a mean between opinion (which concerns our realm) and intelligence. Cf. Simplicius, in De An. p. 309, 20-22 Hayduck, where Iamblichus ranks δόξα with the irrational life.

[26]Both passages are cited by Smith (47 n. 10). See also Dillon (41-42 and 43-44). Smith (47-50) presents several passages from Porphyry's works that show that Porphyry did distinguish between soul and intellect. However, Smith (48) points out two important passages that suggest a reason for Iamblichus' ambivalent remarks about Porphyry (p. 365, 17-19). The first is from the Symmikta Zetemata (ap. Nemesius, De Natura Hominis 135, 7, 11 Matthaei): "sometimes the soul is in itself, whenever it thinks rationally (λογίζηται); but at other times it is in the intellect, whenever it thinks intellectually (νοῇ)." The second is from the De Regressu Animae (Fr. 10, p. 37*, 24-25):

the intellectual soul "is able to become consubstantial with the
paternal mind." Nevertheless, as Smith (50) concludes, the other
evidence shows that Porphyry distinguished soul and intellect.
"Moreover the evidence for conflating them occurs in the context
of spiritual ascent and . . . it would be invalid to deduce
ontological identity from spiritual union." Smith blames
Iamblichus' misunderstanding of Porphyry's view on "a failure to
discern the distinction between these two spheres."

[27]See Smith (47 n. 10) and Wallis (119-120).

[28]See Wallis (113).

[29]See Smith (49 and 47 n. 10) and Wallis (113).

[30]See Festugière (203 n. 3) and the passages cited there.
See also Dillon (43-44).

[31]See Festugière (204 nn. 2 and 3) and Dillon (44).

[32]See the works cited by des Places (172-173 n. 1),
especially Lewy (212 n. 143).

[33]For the material in brackets, see Festugière (248
nn. 1 and 3).

[34]For the equating of this phrase with the rational life,
see Festugière (248 n. 1), where he compares De An. I, p. 375-
18-20. See also Festugière's note on that passage (211 n. 2).

[35]For the appropriate textual references in Porphyry's
De Regressu Animae, see Smith (57-58) and Festugière (80-81
and 247 n. 2). Cf., Dodds (304-305).

[36]See Dillon's note to this fragment (243-244). See
also In Phaedrum Fr. 7 and Dillon's note (255-256), where he
cites De An. I, p. 380, 23-26.

[37]A.D. Nock (XCIV and n. 223) compares Sallustius XXI,
p. 36, 13-14: disembodied souls "administer the whole cosmos
with the gods" (τὸν ὅλον κόσμον συνδιοικοῦσιν ἐκείνοις).

[38]Smith (67) thinks that Iamblichus and Proclus misunder-
stood "the limitations of Porphyry's theory" on the dissolution
of the vehicle and irrational soul. According to Smith, they
"thought that the irrational or lower soul of every single man
would be dissolved after death. The dissolution . . . is the
reward of the philosopher alone and is, no doubt, a rare phenomenon."
But, as has been shown, Iamblichus held a similar belief about
theurgists. They alone, and in small numbers, could escape from
this realm into the higher realms. Surely Iamblichus, at least,
understood Porphyry's point. What Iamblichus criticized was the
dissolution of anyone's vehicle and irrational soul. Smith's

second point, that "Proclus' argument [in] In Tim. iii 235 that
Porphyry's idea would do away with Hades and the traditional
punishments is exaggerated," cannot be turned against Iamblichus.
Iamblichus, like Porphyry, believed that some humans would not
undergo punishment in Hades (De An. I, p. 456, 16-19).

II.   The Human Soul's Connection to the Good

In section I, it was shown that Iamblichus believed that
the vehicle of the soul was immortal and existed intact when the
rational soul separated from it. Such a view differed both from
Porphyry's (that the vehicle was dispersed into the universe) and
from Proclus' (that the rational soul was always attached to a
vehicle).[1]

Two questions arise. First, why does Iamblichus hold this
unique opinion? As was suggested in section I, this question is best
answered by considering the importance and place of theurgy in
Iamblichus' philosophy. Such a study will also answer the second
question: what becomes of the vehicle of the soul when the rational
soul separates from it? Dillon has raised this question and could
come to no satisfactory answer. He says of the irrational soul
(which is housed in the vehicle and like the vehicle is immortal):[2]

> In the purity of the noetic world, it must inevitably
> have been an embarrassment. The physical world being
> eternal, it could stay on eternally in the atmosphere
> as a daemon of some grade, but this is not made clear
> in the surviving evidence.

Before answering these two questions, two preliminary studies
must be made. This section will deal with the role of the so-called
"greater kinds:" what they are, how they differ from human souls
and from one another, and what their role is in Iamblichus' metaphysical and religious systems. In the third section, the soul's
descent into this realm will be discussed. Then in the fourth, the
above two questions about the vehicle's immortality will be considered.

In order to find out more about the nature of the ethereal
vehicle and about the human soul's relationship to it, it will be

necessary to turn to what Iamblichus calls "the greater kinds."[3]
In the De Anima, these include gods, angels, demons, and heroes (I,
p. 378, 3-4 and p. 455, 3-4). In the De Mysteriis, Iamblichus adds
archangels, two types of archon, and purified souls (e.g., II 3,
pp. 70, 17-71, 8). The point of these numerous entities is to fill
the encosmic realm with beings helpful to humans. They both separate
humans from the gods and, at the same time, provide a vital link to
the gods (cf., e.g., De Myst. I 5).

Iamblichus believes that the greater kinds have vehicles
(De An. I, p. 379, 20-22). According to Proclus,[4] the vehicle made
the soul encosmic. For Iamblichus, part of what differentiates the
encosmic gods from the hypercosmic gods is the vehicle. The encosmic
gods are "material and embrace matter in themselves and set it in
order." The hypercosmic gods "are completely separated from matter
and transcend it" (De Myst. V 14, p. 217, 6-8). Although the
encosmic gods are material, they are "unmixed with any material
elements" (De Myst. V 4, p. 202, 4-5) and are, rather, ethereal
(p. 202, 12).[5] The vehicle of the soul was, as stated in section I,
ethereal.

There are several characteristics shared by all the greater
kinds with regard to their vehicles. First, they are separate from
and external to their vehicles. As Iamblichus says, the greater
kinds "do not exist in their bodies but rule them from the outside
(ἔξωθεν)" (De Myst. I 8, p. 24, 2-4) and "being in themselves
separate (χωριστά) from and unmixed with bodies, they pre-exist"
their bodies (p. 24, 11-12).[6] Second, the celestial gods "are not
surrounded (περιέχονται) by their bodies . . . but surround

(περιέχουσι) their bodies by means of their divine lives and energies" (De Myst. I 17, pp. 50, 16-51, 1).[7] They are also said to ride upon (ἐπιβαίνειν) their bodies.[8] Third, the bodies provide neither impediment to the intellections of the greater kinds nor any loss to the greater kinds themselves.[9] Fourth, the greater kinds are impassive.[10]

These common characteristics emphasize the difference not between the greater kinds themselves (since they all share these characteristics) but between the greater kinds and embodied human souls. There is a different kind of relationship, therefore, between the greater kinds and their vehicles, on the one hand, and between human souls and their vehicles, on the other. And this difference exists even though the vehicles of both the greater kinds and humans are ethereal. The difference lies, therefore, not in the astral bodies but in the soul.

As noted in section I, Iamblichus separated the human soul from all souls above it.[11] His theory separates the soul from intellect "since it is generated second after intellect in a separate hypostasis . . . and separates it also from all the greater kinds" (De An. I, p. 365, 22-26).[12] The descending order that Iamblichus envisions is given in In Parm. Fr. 2. According to Iamblichus, the first hypothesis of Plato's Parmenides dealt with god and the gods, the second with noetic entities, the third with the greater kinds, and the fourth with rational souls. Clearly, the greater kinds are of a different order of reality from human souls.

But the souls of the greater kinds differ not only from

human souls but also from one another. For, although all the
greater kinds have vehicles, the relationship between soul and
vehicle is not the same for all of them, as Iamblichus states in
De An. I, p. 379, 18-25:

> The souls of the gods convert their divine bodies, which
> imitate intellect, into their own intellectual substance.
> The souls of other divine kinds, as each soul is ranked,
> thus it guides its vehicle. Purified and perfect souls
> enter into bodies in a pure manner without passions and
> without being deprived of their intellectual capacity
> (τοῦ νοεῖν), but opposite souls enter oppositely.

The words "as each is ranked" (ὡς ἕκασται ἐτάχθησαν) make explicit
the typical Iamblichean hierarchy. The further the progression
downward from gods to souls, the more the relationship between soul
and vehicle deteriorates.

In De An. I, p. 372, 15-22, Iamblichus distinguishes the
acts (ἔργα) of the different souls of the greater kinds. The acts
of universal souls are perfect (παντελῆ), those of divine souls are
pure and immaterial (ἄχραντα καὶ ἄυλα), those of demons are active
(δραστήρια), those of heroes are great (μεγάλα), and those of
animals and men are of a mortal nature (θνητοειδῆ). As Dillon (44)
states: "if the acts are different, the souls are different."

In De An. I, pp. 372, 26-373, 8, Iamblichus, arguing
against Plotinus and Amelius, says that there are different grades
of soul issued in "first, second, and third processions (προόδους)."
Thus higher, more divine souls come from the first processions,
while human souls are from the later processions. As Dillon (45)
notes, the mention of "processions" here is reminiscent of In Tim.
Fr. 82. In this fragment, Iamblichus is concerned with the mixing
bowl of Plato's Timaeus 41d. Plato says that the Demiurge returns

"to the mixing bowl, in which he mixed and mingled the soul of
the universe, and mixing he poured the remainders from the time
before." For Iamblichus, this mixing bowl is a life-producing
cause (ζωόγονος αἰτία) that embraces all life (ζωῆς) and sustains
itself by means of demiurgic logoi. These logoi[13]

> penetrate through all life and through all the soul-orders
> and . . . allot to each soul within its proper sphere
> (λήξει) suitable measures of coherence (μέτρα τῆς συνοχῆς
> πρέποντα), to the original souls primal measures because
> of their first mixture, and to those who are mixed in the
> second session secondary measures; for according as is
> their rank (τάξιν) relative to each other, such is the
> procession (πρόοδον) from the mixing bowl which they are
> allotted, receiving thence the defining bounds of life
> (τοὺς τῆς ζωῆς ὅρους).

In In Tim. Fr. 83, Iamblichus' interpretation of Plato's
phrase "the remainders from the time before" is given. Iamblichus'
opinion is contrasted with the opinions of those who hold that the
"remainders" are what remain of the middle kinds (μέσα γένη).
Iamblichus stresses not the similarity between those middle kinds
(presumably, the demons, heroes, etc. between the gods and human
souls) but the differences. He thinks that the classes of divine
souls (θείων ψυχῶν γένεσις) have a "separated transcendence"
(ἐξηρημένη ὑπεροχή).

From these different fragments, the outline of Iamblichus'
position becomes clear. The souls of the greater kinds differ from
one another by virtue of their particular procession from the mixing
bowl. The highest souls--those of the gods--are the most pure and
completely transcend the lower ranks. The rest of the greater
kinds are less pure.

Nevertheless, although it is clear enough that the different
classes of soul differ from one another, the exact cause of that

difference is not clear. The problem[14] centers around Iamblichus'
phrase "suitable measures of coherence" in In Tim. Fr. 82, line 7
and the referent of γένεσιν in Fr. 83, line 7. Dillon (378),
citing Proclus In Tim. III, pp. 252, 9-256, 21, thinks that the phrase
in Fr. 82 refers to "different proportions of οὐσία, ταυτότης and
ἑτερότης for divine, daemonic, and individual human souls respectively
(254, 4f.)." According to Dillon (379), the word γένεσιν in Fr. 83
therefore "refers . . . to the categories of ὄν, ταυτόν and θάτερον
rather than any class of angels or daemons, and Iamblichus wishes
the divine souls to be made up of components of a different degree
of purity from those of individual souls." Thus, according to Dillon's
theory, the classes of soul differ from each other by a predominance
of a different characteristic in each type of soul. However, in the
section of Proclus' commentary upon which Dillon's argument is
based, Proclus clearly states he is giving his own particular view:
ἐμῇ μαντείᾳ, 252, 9 and ἐμὴ μαντεία, 256, 20. For, although some
of Proclus' argument is based upon Iamblichean principles (e.g.,
that the soul is "the mean between true essence and generation,"
254, 14-15), he is drawing a conclusion that is uniquely his own.
It seems proper, therefore, to conclude that Proclus' thoughts differed
from Iamblichus' in this matter.

Iamblichus' view can be seen in De Myst. I 5. The point
of the chapter is not that each class of soul has a different
predominant characteristic, but, on the contrary, that each class
has a different amount of one characteristic, essence. Iamblichus
begins (p. 15, 5-11) by differentiating two kinds of Good: the Good
beyond essence (ἐπέκεινα τῆς οὐσίας) and the Good in accordance with

essence or the essential Good (κατ' οὐσίαν ὑπάρχον). Iamblichus
continues:

> I mean that essence which is most ancient and honorable
> and is incorporeal in itself, the special property
> (ἰδίωμα ἐξαίρετον) of the gods which exists in all the
> classes around them and which, on the one hand, preserves
> their proper apportionment and rank (διανομὴν καὶ τάξιν)
> and does not detach them from this [apportionment and
> rank] and, on the other hand, exists in all of them in
> the same way.

According to this passage, Iamblichus believes that the
essential Good is present to all the greater kinds but that it is
present in such a way that it preserves the individual rank of each.
At the same time, however, the essential Good is present to each of
them in the same way. The distinction that Iamblichus wishes to
make becomes clearer in what follows (pp. 15, 12-16, 5). Here
Iamblichus discusses disembodied human souls existing (like the
greater kinds) in vehicles in the cosmos. Iamblichus describes these
human souls by three characteristics, all linked by the Greek
conjunction καί: "souls who rule their bodies [i.e., their ethereal
vehicles] and control and care for these bodies and are ranked before
generation, permanent in themselves" (ψυχαῖς δὲ ταῖς ἀρχούσαις τῶν
σωμάτων καὶ προηγουμέναις αὐτῶν τῆς ἐπιμελείας καὶ πρὸ τῆς γενέσεως
τεταγμέναις ἀιδίοις καθ' ἑαυτάς). To these souls neither the
essential Good nor the Good before essence is present. Rather, they
have a retention (ἐποχή) and possession (ἕξις) of the essential Good.

Iamblichus' point is that the greater kinds (gods, demons,
angels, heroes) participate in the essential Good directly and in
the same way, whereas human souls do not participate directly in
the essential Good although they do have some lesser relation to it.

Furthermore, although all the greater kinds participate directly in the essential Good, there is some inequality whereby the different greater kinds receive different ranks or allotments.

Before considering this latter distinction, however, it will be necessary to turn to Festugière's interpretation of De Myst. I 5.[15] According to Festugière, this chapter of the De Mysteriis is Hermetic in tone. Therefore, he sees in Iamblichus' progression from the Good beyond essence to the human soul a typically Hermetic hierarchy. Thus, he takes the Good beyond essence as the first god and the essential Good as the second god. Thus far there is no problem, but Festugière goes on to make the essence itself the third principle ("le Premier Intelligible"). He then equates the gods and "all the kinds around them" (p. 15, 8) not with the visible gods and other greater kinds but with the intelligible gods. Finally, Festugière interprets the "souls who rule bodies" (p. 15, 12) as "the souls who govern the heaven and the stars," i.e., visible gods,[16] and those souls "ranked before generation, permanent in themselves" (p. 15, 13-14) as "human souls before generation."

There are several problems with Festugière's interpretation of De Myst. I 5. First, there is no reason to assume that Iamblichus is promulgating a Hermetic universe here. Festugière's assumption that this is a Hermetic view is based upon the true Hermetic view given in De Myst. VIII 2.[17] However, there are certain differences between that chapter and this. The first difference is that the system delineated in VIII 2 is explicitly said to be by Hermes (p. 262, 9) whereas in book I, Hermes has not been mentioned since chapter 2 (p. 5, 15). Furthermore, although VIII 2 does include a reference to the One and to a second god who is a "monad from the- One"

(p. 262, 4), this second god is prior to essence (προούσιος καὶ

ἀρχὴ τῆς οὐσίας, p. 262, 4-5) and not the Good κατ'οὐσίαν of I 5.

In VIII 2, essence itself (ἡ οὐσιότης καὶ ἡ οὐσία, p. 262, 5-6)

is the third deity, the first principle of the noetic realm, and is

said to originate from the second principle (ἀπ'αὐτοῦ, p. 262, 5);

in I 5, it is not given as a third, vertical emanation but as a

horizontal extension of the Good (i.e., essence exists on the same

plane as the Good). Thus, although there is certainly a correspondence

between the hierarchies expressed in I 5 and VIII 2, the systems

delineated are not the same.

If the metaphysics of VIII 2 is Hermetic, it is certain that

I 5 presents a typically Iamblichean-neoplatonic interpretation.

Dillon (29-39) has organized all the important fragments of Iamblichus

concerning the realm of the One and the noetic realm. A relationship

between these fragments and De Myst. I 5 can be seen. In the realm

of the One, Iamblichus posited three Ones: παντελῶς ἄρρητον, τὸ

ἀπλῶς ἕν, and τὸ ἕν ὄν.   In I 5, he mentions only the latter two,[18]

i.e., the Good beyond essence is τὸ ἀπλῶς ἕν and the essential Good

is τὸ ἕν ὄν. Now, in Iamblichean philosophy, every realm consists

of three moments: ἀμέθεκτος, μετεχόμενος, and κατὰ μέθεξιν or

ἐν σχέσει.[19] The third moment of one realm is the first moment of

the realm below it.[20] Thus, the "One existent" is both the third or

lowest moment of the realm of the One and the first or highest moment

of the noetic realm. As Dillon (35) states: "they are to be dis-

tinguished only for the purposes of exposition." Thus, in De Myst.

I 5, they are not distinguished as separate entities, whereas in VIII

2 Iamblichus can separate them for the sake of argument and agree
both with the Hermetic texts and with his own theories. In I 5,
however, the One existent or the essential Good is considered as a
single entity that is the special property of the gods. Festugière
is wrong, therefore, not only in considering I 5 Hermetic but also
in separating the essential Good from essence itself.

If this argument is correct, it follows that Festugière's
equating of the gods of I 5, p. 15, 7 with the invisible gods is
no longer necessary. Iamblichus here is not showing the effect
of the Good upon all levels of reality; he is arguing that the
different classes of soul partake differently of the essential Good.
He can, therefore, omit the noetic realm entirely (except, of course,
for its highest moment, the essential Good itself) and pass
on to the visible realm and to the greater kinds. Moreover, when
Iamblichus sets out his argument in I 4, p. 14, 15-18, he says:

> If one considers analogously the similarity of the
> mentioned [greater kinds] , such as the many classes
> among the gods (θεοῖς) and then those among the
> demons and heroes, and finally of souls, it would be
> possible for him to distinguish the peculiar nature
> (ἰδιότητα) of each of them.

Here the word θεοῖς (as its position at the head of the list of
demons, heroes, and souls shows) must refer to the highest form of
the greater kinds, viz., the visible gods. It would be most odd,
then, for Iamblichus to switch its referent and to use the word
θεῶν to refer to the invisible gods just nine lines later. Indeed,
throughout these early chapters of book I, in which Iamblichus is
concerned with the relations between the greater kinds, it is the
visible gods that are discussed.[21]

In De Myst. I 19, Iamblichus discusses the connection between the invisible and visible gods. Here he touches on the relation of both to the One, and it becomes clear that the visible gods do have a special relationship with the One similar to the relationship explained in I 5. After explaining that the visible gods have their principles in the noetic realm (p. 57, 7-8), are unmixed with the sensible realm (p. 57, 10-12), and exist together with the invisible gods (p. 57, 12-13), Iamblichus continues by stating that the bodies of the visible gods derive from the noetic paradigms and are established (ἵδρυται) in them (pp. 57, 14-58, 7). They are linked by their noeric energies and mutual participation in the forms, are united by the incorporeal essence (ἄυλος οὐσία καὶ ἀσώματος, cp. οὐσίαν . . . οὖσαν ἀσώματον, I 5, p. 15, 6-7), and are brought together by the procession from the One, the ascent to the One, and the power of the One (p. 58, 8-17). The visible gods remain in the One of the invisible gods, and the invisible gods give their unity to the visible (p. 60, 5-8). Iamblichus concludes (p. 60, 11-15):

> The visible gods are outside of bodies and for this reason are in the noetic realm, and the noetic gods because of their infinite unity embrace in themselves the visible gods, and both are such through a common union and a single energy. And this is a privilege of the gods' cause and order (τῆς τῶν θεῶν αἰτίας καὶ διακοσμήσεως . . . ἐξαίρετον, cp. θεῶν ἰδίωμα ἐξαίρετον, I 5, p. 15, 7-8), on account of which the same unity of all things extends from on high to the end of the divine order.

As this final passage makes clear, the One (or essential Good of I 5) unites the invisible and visible gods to one another and to all the greater kinds. However, the invisible and visible gods are more directly linked to the One and, hence, to one another. It is true that the visible gods' relation to the One comes about

through their union with the invisible gods, but this union is far
more direct than that of the visible gods to the sublunar realm
(which they completely transcend).

There is one more verbal point of similarity between De Myst.
I 19 and I 5 which points to translating θεῶν in I 5 as "visible gods."
In I 19, pp. 59, 1-60, 8, while discussing how the connection between
the invisible and visible gods is superior to the connection between
lower entities (such as soul and body), Iamblichus divides the
category θεῶν into three parts (pp. 59, 15-60, 2):

> With regard to the gods (θεῶν), their rank (τάξις)
> exists in the union of them all. Both the primary and
> secondary classes (γένη) of them and those many classes
> grown around them (τὰ περὶ αὐτὰ φυόμενα) are all united
> in the One, and the all (πᾶν) in them is the One, and
> beginning, middle, and end coexist in the One itself.

The primary classes are, of course, the invisible gods, the secondary
the visible gods. "Those grown around them," i.e., around the
secondary or visible gods, must be the greater kinds. This passage,
therefore, echoes I 5, p. 15, 6-9, which states that the essential
Good is the special property of the gods (θεῶν) and "of all the
classes existing around them" (τὰ γένη τὰ περὶ αὐτοὺς ὄντα). Thus,
not only do both passages speak of the special unity existing between
the gods and the greater kinds, on the one hand, and between the
gods and the One, on the other, but also the reference to "classes
existing around" the gods shows that Iamblichus in both passages
refers to the greater kinds and to their connection to the visible
gods. Thus, the word (θεῶν) in I 5 must refer to the visible gods
since it is to them that the greater kinds are immediately connected.

Finally, returning to Festugière's argument, there seems
little need to consider the phrase "the souls who rule bodies" (I 5,

p. 15, 12) as the celestial gods. For, as has been shown, the celestial gods have already been discussed, and essence has been called their ἰδίωμα ἐξαίρετον. Therefore, the celestial gods cannot be the souls of line 12 since the essential Good is not present to these souls (lines 14-15).

Festugière's interpretation of De Myst. I 5, therefore, is incorrect on several counts. Now that the correct hierarchy of that chapter has been established, it is time to return to the difference between the greater kinds that is delineated there.

Iamblichus continues (p. 16, 6-7) with the words: "the beginning and end in the greater kinds being such." It is now clear that these words refer to the visible gods, who participate directly in the essential Good, and to disembodied human souls, who do not.

Iamblichus then explains the role of demons and heroes in this hierarchy (pp. 16, 7-17, 19). They are both ranked above souls (ὑψηλοτέραν . . . τῆς τῶν ψυχῶν τάξεως). Heroes completely excel (παντελῶς . . . ὑπερέχουσαν) souls but are attached to them through a similar kind of life (ζωῆς ὁμοειδῆ συγγένειαν). Demons are suspended from (ἐξηρτημένην) the gods but are greatly inferior to them. Thus Iamblichus gives their position in the hierarchy. He goes on to give their function. Demons are not primary (πρωτουργόν) but subservient to the gods and make the gods' Good evident. Both demons and heroes complete (συμπληροῦνται) the bond between gods and souls, making a single continuity (συνέχειαν) from the highest to the lowest. They carry both the procession from the gods to souls and the ascent from souls to gods, and make all things agreeable and

harmonious for all by receiving the causes of all things from the
gods.

These middle classes of soul, therefore, are intermediaries
between humans and gods. They have a direct link through the gods
to the One, and they can transfer that Good from the One to human
souls. Thus, the puzzling earlier section of De Myst. I 5--in which
Iamblichus claims that the greater kinds are all linked to the One
in the same way but, at the same time, partake of it in such a way
that each class is ranked differently--can now be explained. The
similarity between gods, demons, and heroes is that they all partake
of the essential Good via the invisible gods. Their difference
is their proximity to that Good. The visible gods are immediately
conjoined to it, the demons through the visible gods, and the heroes
through the demons. On this theory, a human soul is so far removed
from the essential Good (both in distance and in allotment) that
one can no longer speak of the soul's direct participation in it.

It must be admitted, of course, that Iamblichus' distinction
is not as clear-cut as it might be. It would have been better if
he had stressed simply the differences between the greater kinds.
However, to Iamblichus' mind, the greater kinds were also similar.
They were all ranked together under the Parmenides' third hypothesis.
As such, they must transcend the human soul, which he placed in the
fourth hypothesis (In Parm. Fr. 2). It was probably this tension in
Iamblichus' philosophy that forced Proclus to give his own explanation
of the Timaeus' mixing bowl. It should, however, be clear by now
that Proclus' explanation was not Iamblichus'.

The "measures of coherence" (μέτρα τῆς συνοχῆς) of In Tim.
Fr. 82, therefore, are not proportions of essence, sameness, and
otherness, as Dillon suspected. Rather, the term συνοχή should be
taken as the particular soul's connection to the One. (Compare the
word (συνέχειαν) in De Myst. I 5, p. 17, 9). Thus, primary souls
(of the visible gods) have greater measures of coherence because
they are closer to and partake more directly of the One. Those classes
of soul mixed next (demons, for example) are further removed from
the One. A more explicit statement of this distinction is made in
De Myst. I 20, pp. 61, 15-62, 3. Here, Iamblichus is explaining the
difference between the visible gods and demons. The visible gods,
he says, who are "united to the noetic gods have the same essence
(ἰδέαν)[22] as they, but the others (i.e., the demons) are far removed
from them in essence (κατὰ τὴν οὐσίαν)."

This doctrine of Iamblichus--that the further down the scale
of being an entity is, the less fully it participates in the One--
seems to be a corollary of a doctrine given in In Alc. Fr. 8. Here
it is given as Iamblichus' δόγμα that[23]

> irrespective of what point a principle begins to operate,
> it does not cease its operation before extending to the
> lowest level; for even if ⟨the influence of a higher
> principle⟩ is stronger, nevertheless the fact of its
> greater separation can create a balancing factor, rendering
> it weaker . . . the influence of the higher principles
> is more piercing, more keenly felt.

Thus, on the theory expressed in this fragment, the essential One
exerts influence all the way down the scale of being. However, the
greater the separation from the One to an entity, the less the One's
effect. This is exactly the case with the effect of the essential
Good upon gods, demons, heroes, and human souls.[24]

If human souls differ from divine souls by virtue of their participation in the essential Good (and not by virtue of having more ἑτερότης), it follows that the phrase θείων ψυχῶν γένεσιν in In Tim. Fr. 83 does not refer "to the categories of ὄν, ταυτόν and θάτερον," as Dillon (379) thinks. Rather, the term γένεσιν should be given its regular meaning of "class." Iamblichus' point in Fr. 83 will then be the same as his point in Fr. 82. For, it is stated in Fr. 83 that Iamblichus "assigns a separated transcendence to the classes comprising (συμπληπτωτικοῖς) the divine souls." In other words, the higher, divine γένερα (such as gods) transcend the lower γένερα (such as souls). This view is similar to that of the processions from the mixing bowl and to that of De Myst. I 5.[25]

From the foregoing argument, it is now clear not only that the different classes of soul differ from one another but also how they differ. It follows that the relationship between a soul and its vehicle deteriorates as the soul participates less fully in the One. A soul, therefore, that is not participating properly (according to its rank) in the One will need external aid or purification in order to become again what it properly should be. Thus, since a human soul partakes of Good via the greater kinds, the human soul needs the help of the greater kinds in order to achieve its highest possible rank. Iamblichus' theory of the different classes of soul and their different participation in the Good dovetails perfectly with his theory of religion. It is time, then, to consider how any soul comes to stand in need of ritual purification.

In De Myst. V 4, pp. 202, 12-203, 8, while arguing that the

gods are not affected by sacrificial exhalations, Iamblichus states

the following about ethereal bodies:

> For it is agreed that the ethereal body is external to any
> opposition (ἐναντιώσεως) is freed from any change (τροπῆς)
> is free from the possibility of changing (μεταβάλλειν)
> into anything else, is completely without tendency toward
> or from the middle because it lacks any such tendency or
> is carried about in a circle (κατὰ κύκλον περιφέρεται) . . .
> For, these ethereal bodies, being ungenerated, do not have
> any power of receiving into themselves change from generated
> things.

This passage proclaims the perfection, unity, and permanence

appropriate to an entity created by the Demiurge himself. There are

two points of note. First, the vehicle is unchangeable, the word

μεταβάλλειν being reminiscent of μεταβλητόν in In Tim. Fr. 81

(discussed in section I, above). This attribute reinforces the

notion of the vehicle's immortality and unity. Second, the natural

movement of the vehicle is circular, imitating the motion of the

planets. This notion of circular movement is consistent with the myth

in Plato's Phaedrus (248a1-b5, especially a3-4: συμπεριηνέχθη

τὴν περιφοράν), where souls in their chariots follow the gods around

the heavens, and with In Tim. Fr. 49, lines 13-14, where Iamblichus

says the spherical vehicle of the human soul is moved in a circle

(κινεῖται κυκλικῶς). It is clear, then, that the appropriate life

for souls in vehicles is to revolve in conjunction with the gods.

The problem posed by the above passage comes from its last

sentence. For, if the ungenerated vehicles are not receptive to

change from generated things, why is purification necessary? The

answer lies in the kind of change that Iamblichus is considering.

Iamblichus' point is that the vehicle, being a creation of the

Demiurge, is eternal and unaltered by material sacrifices. Such
entities are not changed by anything material, i.e., vehicles remain
eternally what they are. No change occurs within them (εἰς ἑαυτά, p.
203, 7). This is not to say, however, that external entities can have
no effect. On the contrary, external material substances do affect
the vehicle, but they cannot change it.

Put another way, the vehicle of every soul (regardless of
the soul's rank) is an ethereal, eternal entity. When the relationship
between the soul and the vehicle is as it should be (as is always the
case with the visible gods), the soul and vehicle revolve together
and the soul enjoys perfect intellection. However, since lower souls
partake less fully of the Good, their relationship with their
vehicles can be affected by material substances.

Several passages in the De Mysteriis help to explain how
this contamination occurs. In I 20, pp. 63, 3-64, 12, Iamblichus
differentiates between gods (both invisible and visible) and demons
by reference to their ruling allotment. The gods rule over the
whole universe, whereas demons have only a partial allotment. The
gods, therefore, are separated from matter, but demons are directly
involved with generation (τῇ γενεσιουργῷ φύσει προσκεῖσθαι).
Iamblichus concludes: "Therefore, the gods are freed from powers
that tend to generation (ῥεπουσῶν εἰς τὴν γένεσιν),[26] but demons
are not entirely pure of them."

Demons, therefore, are enmeshed in matter. In De Myst.
II 5, a similar distinction is found. In certain theurgic rites, the
highest ranks of souls (gods, archangels, and angels) lead human
souls away from generation. The lower ranks (beginning with the

demons) do not. Indeed, demons "drag them down into nature" (p. 79,
8-9). Furthermore, Iamblichus attributes the purity and stability
of an εἰκών in such a rite to the highest ranks, and to the demons
and lower ranks he assigns "what is carried, unstable, and filled
with foreign natures" (ἀλλοτρίων φύσεων,ͺ pp. 79, 19-80, 2).
This involvement with material elements leads to a different commixture (συμμίξεως, p. 80, 4) for these inferior souls. In p. 80,
4-14,[27] Iamblichus indicates that the commixture becomes more material
as one progresses down through the different classes of soul. Vapors
that subsist in the region under the moon (ἀτμοὶ περικόσμιοι) are
mixed with demons, combinations of genesiourgic pneumata with heroes.
The hylic archons are filled full (ἀνάμεστοι) of material liquids
(ἰχῶρες), and human souls are filled (ἀναπίμπλανται) with excessive
stains and foreign pneumata.

Demons and other inferior souls, therefore, become
contaminated by matter. In human souls, this material covering
becomes its corporeal body.[28] And this corporeal body is a greater
burden for human souls than the vehicle is for the gods. For,
Iamblichus says in De Myst. V 2, p. 200, 5-9, the celestial gods
receive neither harm nor impediment to their intellections from
their bodies, whereas human souls receive both from theirs. Furthermore, in De Myst. V 3, p. 201, 1-5, Iamblichus states that the union
of soul and body causes heaviness and pollution (βαρύτητα καὶ μιασμόν),
luxury (ἡδυπάθειαν), and many other diseases (νοσήματα) in the soul.

An explanation for the human body's ability to cause such
harm to the soul can be glimpsed in De Myst. I 18. Here Iamblichus

is discussing the cause of evil in the world. The cause is not the gods (because they are good) but matter's participation in the divine good. The gods' bodies have infinitely great powers (ἀμηχάνους . . . (δυνάμεις, p. 53, 6-7), some of which go forth into the realm of generation. Although these powers are for the good of this realm, this realm tends to distort them. It receives the One of the gods self-contradictorily and partially (μαχομένως καὶ μεριστῶς, p. 54, 3). Iamblichus continues (p. 54, 6-11 and p. 55, 3-6):

> Just as something begotten partakes of being by means of generation (γεννητῶς) and the body partakes of the incorporeal corporeally, so too physical and material things in generation partake of the immaterial and ethereal bodies that are above nature and generation in a disordered and faulty way . . . Participation (μετάληψις), the commixture of material elements with immaterial emanations, and the receiving in one way down here of something given in another way become the cause of the great difference in secondary entities.

Thus, there is something in matter itself which causes matter to receive the Good emanating from the gods (via their immaterial vehicles) in an altered manner. Matter, therefore, adhering to the soul's vehicle can cause distortion to the soul itself. For, it can prevent the soul from its proper manner of participating in the Good.[29]

It follows that purification is required to remove the stain caused by matter. Once the material pollution is removed from the soul's vehicle, nothing prevents the soul--with the help of the gods-- from participating in the Good in an appropriate manner. Furthermore, as is manifest from De An. I, p. 379, 23-25 (quoted at the beginning of this section), once the soul has been purified, it can return to a human body and not be made impure by it.

It should be clear, then, that there are two forces at
work that determine a soul's purity. First, there is the essential
Good. According to a soul's rank, the soul participates directly
or through the intermediaries of the gods and greater kinds in the
Good. The higher the soul is ranked, the more direct its participation. The lower it is ranked, the more it needs the help of
intermediaries. Second, there is the contamination caused by matter.
As long as the soul is stained by material additions, it remains
unable to partake properly in the essential Good because matter
distorts the Good's emanation. Theurgical purification, then, acts
in two ways. First, it removes the contamination caused by matter.
Second, it re-unites the soul to the Good by means of the divine
intermediaries. The greater kinds, accordingly, perform two services
for the soul. First, they bring the essential Good from the gods
to the human soul. Second, they act as intermediaries in the
soul's purification, leading the soul up to the gods.[30]

Notes to Section II

[1]See, e.g., El. Th. 196 and Dodd's note (300). Proclus believed that there were two vehicles, see Dodds (320) and Kissling (323-324).

[2]Dillon (376, cf. 250-251).

[3]Usually termed κρείττονα γένη, as in De An. I, p. 365, 27; 377, 18; 378, 3; 455, 3, and in De Myst. I 3, p. 8, 15; I 4, p. 12, 1; I 10, p. 33, 16, and passim. Note that κρείττονα γένη is also used by Proclus when he refers to Iamblichus' placing of these greater kinds in the third hypothesis (see Iamblichus' In Parm. Fr. 2, line 8). The terms πρεσβύτερα γένη (De An. I, p. 365, 11) and θεῖα γένη (De An. I, p. 379, 20-21 and De Myst. I 8, p. 23, 15) are also used. For a useful summary of these greater kinds in the De Mysteriis, see Dillon (49-52).

[4]Proclus, In Tim. III, p. 298, 27-28; cf. 235, 27-30. The first passage is cited by Kissling (324).

[5]According to De Myst. V 12, p. 215, 8-11, "the bodily (σωματοειδές) vehicle that is subordinate to demons is not from matter, elements, or any other body known to us." Although Iamblichus does not say so, it is clear that this "unknown" substance is ether. Kissling (326), citing this passage, thinks that "Iamblichus accepts the theory of the daemonical πνεῦμα but is unable to define its nature except by negative statements." However, Kissling's position is overturned by Iamblichus' assertions about the vehicle in general (De Myst. V 4, pp. 202, 12-203, 8, quoted below) and about the demon's vehicle in particular (De Myst. V 10, p. 212, 5-6): The demon's vehicle "is unchangeable, without passion, luminous, and in need of nothing (ἄτρεπτον . . . ἀπαθὲς αὐγοειδές τε καὶ ἀνενδεές)." Note also that since ethereal bodies are not material in the way human bodies are, they are sometimes called "immaterial" (De Myst. I 18, p. 54, 9-10; see also I 17, p. 52, 12-13 and 16-17, where they are "in a certain way incorporeal"). Since it is the nature and purpose of this "fifth element" to unite the material to the immaterial, it itself partakes of both materiality and immateriality. The resulting confusion is inherent in Neoplatonism.

[6]In De Myst. I 19, p. 60, 11-12, the visible gods are outside of (ἔξω) bodies. For separateness, see I 20, p. 63, 13: "the gods are completely separated (κεχωρισμένοι) from" bodies. Cp. V 14, p. 218, 9-10, where the gods, though as much as possible separated (χωριστοί) from matter (i.e., ὕλη), are nonetheless present with it.

[7]Cp. V 14, p. 217, 6 and 218, 11, where the material gods surround matter (τὴν ὕλην περιέχοντας and περιέχουσιν αὐτήν).

[8]Cf. I 20, p. 63, 12-13 and V 2, p. 200, 6. Cp. V 14,

p. 217, 12 where the material gods "ride upon" matter. The word ἐπιβαίνειν means both "ride upon" and "preside over" in all of these contexts. Thus, des Places translates the word in these three passages by chevaucher, gouverner, and trôner respectively.

[9]No impediment: I 17, p. 51, 3-5: "the body of the celestial gods does not impede their intellectual and incorporeal perfection;" I 20, p. 63, 16: the body "provides no impediment to" the visible god; V 2, p. 200, 7-8: the heavenly gods receive "no impediment toward their intellections" from their bodies. No loss: I 20, p. 63, 13-15: "Having a concern for bodies does not bring any loss (ἐλάττωσιν) to those gods who are served by the body."

[10]See I 10, pp. 33, 15-34, 6 and pp. 36, 6-37, 2; V 4, p. 204, 7-13; V 10, p. 212, 3-7. Cf. I 4, pp. 11, 16-12, 13.

[11]Dillon (41-45) cites De An. I, pp. 365, 7-366, 11 and pp. 372, 4-373, 8 as well as In Tim. Frr. 82 and 83 in his discussion of Iamblichus' philosophy concerning the soul. The present discussion draws from Dillon's with certain modifications and additions.

[12]See also, with Festugière (185 n. 5), De An. I, p. 367, 3-4: the soul is "generated from all the more divine kinds."

[13]The translation is Dillon's (195-196).

[14]As Dillon (45, 377-379) notes.

[15]Festugière (48-50). He is followed by des Places (46 and n. 2).

[16]Festugière (49 n. 3), although later in the same note he admits that "il est possible que la phrase de Jamblique désigne la seule classe des âmes humaines qui, au ciel, avant la generation, gouvernent les corps célestes et le monde en tant qu'auxiliaires des âmes divines."

[17]Festugière seems to be following W. Scott (28-102) in this. However, Scott does not expressly include De Myst. I 5 among his fragments, although he does indicate that more chapters than the first two of book I should be included. See Scott (31, line 6).

[18]Scott (52-53) thinks that the absence of the first One from De Myst. I 5 proves that the author of the De Mysteriis was not Iamblichus. However, in I 5, Iamblichus discusses the realm of the One only to show its effect upon the different classes of soul. Since the first One is completely transcendent and has no direct effect upon the lower realms, mention of it is unnecessary.

[19]See Dillon (33 and 335-336).

[20]See Dillon (35).

[21] Such is the case for I 5 as well. See, for example, p. 16, 12-14: demons are "suspended from the gods" (τῶν θεῶν ἐξηρτημένην). Cf. p. 17, 7-8: "these middle genera (i.e., heroes and demons) make up the common bond of gods and souls;" and p. 18, 4-6, at the conclusion of the argument: "you will complete the answer concerning the peculiar natures of gods, demons, heroes, and souls . . ." From all of these citations, it is clear that the word θεῶν refers to the highest of the greater kinds, the visible gods.

[22] As des Places (75-76 n. 1) states: "ἰδέα et οὐσία sont quasi synonymes." He compares De Myst. X 5. See also des Places (222), where he cites W. Scott (92). Scott thinks that ἰδέα is "the logical 'essence' of a thing." It must be remembered, however, that for Iamblichus a thing's essence is not only what the thing is but also something derived from ὄν the first member of the noetic triad. A thing's essence must come from a pre-existing essence.

[23] The translation is Dillon's (83).

[24] Iamblichus may have adopted his doctrine (of superior souls being more closely connected to the One) from Plotinus, Enn. IV.3.6.27-34. There Plotinus is discussing Plato's Tim 41d4-7, where the Demiurge returns to the mixing bowl and mixes the souls "no longer the same as before, but second and third in purity (δεύτερα καὶ τρίτα)." Plotinus quotes these final three Greek words and argues that they must be understood to mean "proximity or distance" with regard to the One.

[25] In In Tim. Fr. 83, the phrase θείων ψυχῶν γένεσιν refers not to all the greater kinds (as the phrase θείοις γένεσι does in De Myst. I 5, p. 16, 7) but to the souls of the visible gods alone. This interpretation is proven by the reference to the "middle classes" (μέσων γενῶν) earlier in the fragment. (Compare γένη μέσα in De Myst. I 5, p. 17, 7.) The transcendency of the gods is frequent in the De Mysteriis. See, e.g., V 2, p. 200, 3-4; V 4, p. 203, 5-6: V 17, p. 222.

[26] For the significance and frequency of the phrase, see des Places (76 n. 1), where he cites Lewy (294 n. 136). Lewy notes that the word ῥέπω "derives from Plato, Phaedr., 247b, 4," i.e., from the Phaedrus myth. Cf. Smith (1 n. 2). Note that in De Myst. V 4, pp. 202, 14-203, 1 (quoted above), the vehicle itself lacks ῥοπή toward and from the middle either because it is ἀρρεπές (probably the case with the visible gods) or because it is carried in a circle. Thus, it seems, the soul's tendency toward generation goes hand in hand with its ceasing its circular motion and with its descent.

[27] Partially quoted with respect to Iamblichus' theory of vestments in section I, above.

[28]According to Dodds (308-309), Proclus believed that demons "have spherical vehicles, but the lower sort have material bodies as well (in Crat. 35.22, Th. Pl. III.(v). 125f.).'' It is probable that Iamblichus held a similar theory. In In Tim. Fr. 80, Iamblichus claims that there is one kind of death for "so-called relational demons" (οἱ κατὰ σχέσιν λεγόμενοι) but that "essential demons" (οἱ κατ' οὐσίαν δαίμονες) are exempt from any such death. These two kinds of demon are discussed by Proclus in In Tim. III, pp. 157, 27-159, 7. For Proclus, the relational demons are the sub-celestial demons (ὑπουράνιοι) and are created both rational and irrational by the sub-celestial gods. For Iamblichus, the relational demons underwent a form of death "like the removal of a chiton" (οἷον χιτῶνος ἀπόθεσιν). This jargon is reminiscent of the "putting aside" of vestments in a soul's reascent. It seems likely, therefore, that Iamblichus believed that relational demons had bodies of vestments, i.e., of material elements gathered in the sublunar realm. These vestments, of course, are separate from the demon's vehicle and could be sloughed off when the demon underwent "death," i.e., when it ascended to a higher τάξις. Proclus' relational demons, however, are merely irrational, not evil. Proclus did not believe in evil demons-- see Nock (lxxviii and lxxix n. 175). Some of Iamblichus' relational demons are probably evil. For, in De Myst. IX 7, p. 282, 3-5, Iamblichus states that evil demons (unlike good ones) have no "ruling allotment" (ἡγεμονικὴν . . . λῆξιν). Relational demons, by the very fact of their close proximity to matter, would have no such λῆξις either. They, like human souls in bodies, lead a more partial existence. See also Lewy (261 n. 8).

[29]It is worth noting that Iamblichus does not believe that matter is inherently evil. Rather, matter simply does not have the power to receive the Good properly. Material envelopes affect not only human souls but also all the souls of the greater kinds up to and including those of demons, as is shown by De Myst. II 5, pp. 80, 15-81, 9. Here Iamblichus states that matter is devoured quickly by the gods, less quickly by the archangels, and that there is a freeing from and a leading away from it by angels. Demons, however, are adorned with matter, and so on down the scale. Thus, Iamblichus' belief in evil demons is probably a corollary of his belief in the distortion caused by matter. Evil demons are evil because they are immersed in matter. For Sallustius' view that there are no evil demons, see Nock (lxxviii-lxxix).

[30]See, for example, De Myst. I 5, p. 16, 16-17: demons "expose the hidden good of the gods into actuality;" and p. 17 12-14: demons and heroes "transport the procession from betters to inferiors and the ascent from inferiors to first natures."

III. The Descent of the Soul

In view of the greater kinds' intermediary role in the
human soul's connection to the Good and in the human soul's reascent,
it is not surprising to find that the greater kinds also play an
intermediary role in the soul's descent into this realm. The purpose
of this section will be twofold. First, the manner in which Iamblichus
conceived the human soul's descent via the gods and greater kinds will
be discussed. Second, Iamblichus' opinion about the impetus for the
soul's descent will be considered: whether the descent is voluntary
or involuntary, whether or not τόλμα is involved.

A. The Process of the Descent

Iamblichus discusses the soul's descent in De An. I, pp. 377,
13-380, 29.[1] He begins in a familar way by setting himself apart
from Plotinus, Porphyry, and Amelius. These three, Iamblichus says,
"make souls enter equally into bodies from the Hypercosmic Soul."
There are two points here: (1) human souls depart from the Hypercosmic
Soul, and (2) all souls are equal when they enter into bodies.

Iamblichus has no disagreement with the first claim. In
In Tim. Fr. 54, he states that both the Soul of the Universe and
the other partial souls originate from the Hypercosmic Soul.[2] It is
with the second claim that he disagrees. As Festugière (216 n. 2)
says, Iamblichus has already argued against the position of Plotinus,
Amelius, and Porphyry concerning the difference between the different
classes of soul at De An. I, pp. 372, 4-373, 8. Furthermore, at
pp. 365, 5-366, 11, Iamblichus again takes a similar stance against
the same three philosophers.[3] Simply put, Iamblichus' contention is
that the souls do not emanate equally (ἐπίσης, p. 377, 14) from the

59

Hypercosmic Soul. Different classes of soul proceed in different and unequal ranks. The human soul is different from the Whole Soul (i.e., the Hypercosmic Soul), from Intellect, and from the greater kinds.

Iamblichus continues (p. 377, 16-29) by giving a summary of the Timaeus' view of the soul's descent. Festugière (216 n. 4) thinks that this passage is "un résumé du Commentaire de Jamblique sur le Timée . . . à propos de Tim. 41e3" and compares Proclus' In Tim. III, pp. 275, 24-279, 2,[4] which he thinks follows Iamblichus' commentary. Although it certainly is true that this passage of the De Anima is based upon Iamblichus' lost Timaeus commentary and that Proclus (in his commentary) agrees with Iamblichus on certain issues concerning the soul's descent, there are also differences between Iamblichus' and Proclus' interpretations of Plato. It will be necessary, therefore, to consider Proclus' exegesis at length—covering his commentary not just on Tim. 41e but also on several other passages—and to try to reconstruct Iamblichus' interpretation, both where he differs from and where he agrees with Proclus.

In De An. I, 377, 16-29, Iamblichus says:

> Very differently the Timaeus seems to make the first generation (πρώτην ὑπόστασιν) of souls, the Demiurge sowing (διασπείροντα) them around all the greater kinds, throughout all heaven, and into all the elements (στοιχεῖα) of the universe. Therefore, the demiurgic sowing (σπορά) of souls will be divided around the divine creations, and the first procession (πρόοδος) of souls exists with it, holding with itself the places receiving the souls: the Whole Soul has the whole cosmos, the souls of the visible gods have the heavenly spheres, and the souls of the elements have the elements themselves. With these the souls are also assigned (συνεκληρώθησαν) in each such allotment (λῆξιν), and from these the descents (κάθοδοι) of souls occur, some souls from some allotments (διακληρώσεων) and others from others, as the arrangement

(διάταξις) of the <u>Timaeus</u> clearly intends to show.

Festugière (258) rightly sees connections between this passage and the beginning of Proclus' chapter of the <u>Timaeus</u> commentary on 41e3: "That the first genesis (πρώτη γένεσις) would be arranged one for all so that none may be slighted by him [i.e., the Demiurge]." Proclus begins by discussing the soul's πρώτη ὑπόστασις: "Souls are essentially supernatural, hypercosmic, and above fate because they hold a first generation (πρώτην ὑπόστασιν) separate from this cosmos" (p. 275, 26-28). Souls become subservient to fate, Proclus says, "by their vehicles and by their allotments (λήξεις), which they are assigned (ἐκληρώσαντο) to administer" (p. 275, 28-29).

Both Proclus and Iamblichus, therefore, see the soul's movement from the hypercosmic realm into generation as occurring in stages. First the soul is above fate and then it becomes subservient to fate. However, there are intermediate stages upon which Festugière does not comment. For, Proclus also says (p. 276, 5-11):

> In order that the souls with their vehicles may come under the domain of fate, they must have a descent (καθόδων) and an association with generation, which is second after the sowing (σποράν). For this [i.e., the sowing] is first, being a sort of second distribution (διανομή) of the vehicles under the divine circulations, just as there occurred a division of the souls themselves into the [divine] souls.

So, for Proclus, there is the πρώτη ὑπόστασις, the distribution,[5] the sowing, the assignment of allotments, then the descent. Iamblichus seems to follow a similar hierarchy in the <u>De Anima</u>, although he omits mention of the distribution of souls and introduces a "first procession."

Festugière (216 n. 4) thinks that, in the De Anima
passage, Iamblichus equates the πρώτη ὑπόστασις with the
demiurgic sowing. Such an equation is impossible. Proclus clearly
differentiates between the two. The πρώτη ὑπόστασις is hypercosmic,
while the sowing is encosmic, occurring around the vehicles of the
gods. Iamblichus, too, believes that the soul is essentially hypercosmic.[6] Moreover, he clearly conceives of the sowing as occurring
in the cosmos since the sowing includes the greater kinds (De An.
I, p. 377, 18).

For both Iamblichus and Proclus, then, the πρώτη ὑπόστασις
differs from the sowing. Iamblichus, therefore, is not equating
the πρώτη ὑπόστασις with the sowing but is contrasting them. His
reason for this particular contrast becomes clear from his In Tim.
Fr. 85. Here Iamblichus is considering what Plato meant by the phrase
"first genesis" (γένεσις πρώτη, Tim. 41e3). For Iamblichus, the
"first genesis" is "the sowing of the vehicles" (τὴν τῶν ὀχημάτων
σποράν).

There is, however, some problem with the meaning of the
phrase "the sowing of the vehicles." Dillon (199) translates it
"the 'sowing' (of souls) into vehicles,"[7] and Festugière (260) as
"l'ensemencement dans les chars." But it has already been seen
that Proclus (who is the source of Iamblichus' fragment) considered
the sowing a "second distribution of souls under the divine
circulations" (In Tim. III, p. 276, 8-9); that is to say, the sowing
is not of the soul into the vehicle but of the soul (with its
vehicle) into the visible gods. And, indeed, Iamblichus says
exactly this in De An. I, p. 377, 19-21: "the demiurgic sowing of

souls will be divided around the divine creations."[8]   It is better,
therefore, to understand the phrase "the sowing of the vehicles"
as the dispersion of souls together with their vehicles around the
gods.

Plato speaks of the first generation in the context of
the Demiurge's speech to souls already placed in their vehicles
(Tim. 41e2-42a3): The Demiurge

> told them the fated laws, that the first genesis would
> be arranged one for all in order that none might be
> slighted by him and that it would be necessary, having
> sown (σπαρείσας) them into each of the organs of time
> appropriate to them, that the most holy of animals be
> born; but human nature being double, that kind would be
> superior which would then be called "male."

To a neoplatonist, there must be something special about this first
generation because it is common to all souls.

Dillon (380-381), believing that Iamblichus considered the
first genesis "the 'sowing' (of souls) into vehicles," argues
that Iamblichus "must then assume all ὀχήματα to be of equal value
. . . Differences in the quality of life must then depend on how good
one's relation is with one's ὄχημα." However, since the first
genesis is the sowing of souls around the gods (and other greater
kinds), Iamblichus has a different point in mind. Proclus (In Tim.
III, p. 280, 19-21) helps to explain what is at issue:

> But they [i.e., the souls] make their first descent when
> they have already been sown around the visible gods in
> order that they might have the gods as saviors (σωτῆρας)
> of their wandering around generation and that they might
> call upon them as their own patrons (προστάτας).

The sowing, therefore, makes each soul fall under its own appropriate god.[9] The sowing, being the first genesis according to
Iamblichus, therefore guarantees to each and every soul a leader god

64

as a means to salvation. In other words, the soul's salvation is attained through the soul's cosmic god, a view very much in harmony with the greater kinds' role discussed in section II, above.

Iamblichus' reason for speaking in the De Anima of the πρώτη ὑπόστασις of souls and the sowing of the souls can now be seen. For him, these two events represent the two primary stages in a soul's life. The πρώτη ὑπόστασις is the rational soul's hypercosmic life when it is separated from the cosmos and from its cosmic ethereal vehicle.[10] The sowing represents the establishment of the soul and its vehicle into the circulation of the soul's cosmic god. As was stated in section II above, this conception of an entourage of souls following the gods around the heavens is based upon Plato's Phaedrus myth. The sowing, therefore, represents the placing of the human soul in its heavenly λῆξις from which it can either rise to the noetic realm or fall into generation.

It also should be noted that the sowing pertains not just to human souls but also to the souls of the other greater kinds below the visible gods. Proclus discusses this matter at In Tim. III, p. 280, 22-32. His argument runs as follows: Plato does not refer only to living things in the earth but also to those "in the other elements" (line 23). Therefore, Plato is considering both humanity and "other living things more divine yet generated" (lines 24-25). This is so because beings that exist for the shortest period of time (ὀλιγοχρονιώτατον) do not exist immediately after eternal beings. There is need of a middle type of being that has a more enduring (διαρκέστερον) span of life (lines 25-28). It is this middle group that Plato calls "the most holy of living things" (Tim.

42a1), by which term Plato means "those able to participate in Intellect and to revert (ἐπιστρέφειν) to the gods" (lines 30-31). Plato refers specifically to humanity in the next sentence of the Timaeus: "human nature being twofold, the superior would be that which then would be called 'male'" (Tim. 42a1-3). This middle group of living beings that is neither eternal nor the shortest-lived of beings is the greater kinds, the link between gods and mortals.

That this is a Iamblichean view is supported by Proclus' commentary upon Tim. 39e10-40a2, where Plato had said:

> And these [i.e., the different living things that must be created] are four: one is the heavenly class of gods, second the winged class that traverses the air, third the class that lives in water, and fourth the class travelling on foot on the land.

Proclus asks to what entities these four groups of living things refer. In his subsequent discussion, he refers to four different opinions. One of these has a distinctly Iamblichean ring (In Tim. III, pp. 107, 30-108, 1):

> Others, looking to facts (πράγματα) say that these refer to gods and to the kinds greater than ourselves because these classes pre-exist mortals and because it is necessary that the Demiurge not make the mortal classes immediately (ἀμέσως) from the divine.

The view that mortals are not immediately joined to the gods but require the greater kinds as intermediaries is, as was seen in section II above, Iamblichean.

Moreover, although Proclus disagrees with the opinion just expressed and follows Syrianus' interpretation (p. 108, 7ff.), he nonetheless does not dismiss this earlier point of view summarily. In fact, Proclus gives it some credit: "Such being the differences among the interpreters we admire the one fond of contemplating the

facts (τὸν φιλοθεάμονα τῶν πραγμάτων)" (p. 108, 5-7). Proclus'
comment suggests the respectful attitude usually held for the
divine Iamblichus.[11]

Furthermore, Iamblichus' own metaphysical system requires
that he read the greater kinds into the Timaeus at this point.
For, Plato states (Tim. 39e3-40a2) that all living things (πάντα
ζῷα) had not yet been made. Plato immediately says that the gods
are made τὴν πλείστην ἰδέαν ἐκ πυρός (Tim. 40a2-3). If the gods are
made from fire, it is only reasonable for a neoplatonist to assume
that the greater kinds follow, in a descending order, in the other
three elements mentioned in Tim. 39e10-40a2.[12] Moreover, as far
as Iamblichus is concerned, the elements mentioned here by Plato
cannot refer to anything corporeal. For, as Dillon has pointed out,[13]
Iamblichus does not believe that Plato mentions matter until Tim.
47e3. Therefore, the entities existing in the elements cannot be
corporeal, and the greater kinds, of course, are incorporeal.
Finally, since Iamblichus believes that the greater kinds exist
above human souls in their own hypostasis (In Parm. Fr. 2), it is
necessary that these beings come into existence before human souls.

For Iamblichus, therefore, the sowing is not just of human
souls and vehicles around their own gods but also of the greater kinds.
It follows that each god has its own following of angels, demons,
heroes, etc. as well as its own entourage of human souls. Moreover,
human souls, since they are ranked after the souls of the greater
kinds, by their very sowing are connected to certain greater kinds
that can aid them in their reascent.

The πρώτη ὑπόστασις and the first genesis (i.e., the

sowing) are linked together in the De Anima, therefore, as repre-
sentative of the first two allotments held by human souls. On the
other hand, Proclus, following Syrianus, disagrees with Iamblichus
(In Tim. III, pp. 278, 9-279, 2). He believes that the first
genesis is the soul's "descent from the noetic realm" (p. 278,
31-32: τὴν ἀπὸ τοῦ νοητοῦ κάθοδον). He argues against Iamblichus
by pointing out that Tim. 42b5-c1 refers to a "second genesis"
(δευτέρᾳ γενέσει) into a woman (p. 278, 28-31 and 292, 12-18).
Unfortunately, it is nowhere recorded what Iamblichus thought about
this "second genesis."

Although Proclus and Iamblichus disagree about the meaning
of Plato's "first genesis," they do agree about the role of the
sowing itself. To a neoplatonist, Plato mentions the sowing twice
in the Timaeus: 41e4-42a4 and 42d4-5. In Proclus' commentary to
the first passage (In Tim. III, pp. 279, 6-280, 32), he makes it clear
again that the sowing is separate from the first genesis. He
argues that although every soul must descend, each soul differs from
others by its being sown into its own leader god. Thus, whereas
Iamblichus had stressed the similarity involved in the sowing of the
soul (i.e., every soul had a leader god to aid it in its reascent),
Proclus chooses to stress the differences inherent in the sowing
(i.e., one soul is solar, another lunar, another mercurial, etc.).
This is not to say that Iamblichus rejected the belief that souls
sown into different gods differed from one another. A closer
inspection of Proclus' In Tim. III, p. 279, 11-30 reveals similarities
with Iamblichus' writings as well.

Proclus admits three sources of difference between the

various human souls. Souls differ from one another by the leader-
ship of a god (lines 11-13), by λόγων προβολαί (lines 13-20), and
by their deliberative choices (προαιρέσεις, lines 20-24). It has
already been argued that Iamblichus accepted the demiurgic sowing of
human souls into those of the gods. The doctrine of the sowing is
the philosophical basis of the neoplatonic theory of astrological
influences on human life.[14] Thus, Iamblichus would have seen the
sowing of souls into the gods as the cause of both similarity and
differences between the souls: similar in that all souls are given
a leader, different in that each leader exerts a different influence
on the souls under its power.[15]

Iamblichus and Proclus, then, would have agreed that souls
having different leader gods tended to differ from one another. It
is difficult to determine, however, to what degree the other two
differences mentioned by Proclus are Iamblichean. Iamblichus did
believe that there were great differences between human souls, and
not all of these differences can be explained simply by stating that
the souls fall under different divinities.[16] Whether he divided
the differences in the way that Proclus does is another matter.

Nevertheless, there is some evidence that Iamblichus made
a point similar to Proclus'. Proclus explains the phrase λόγων
προβολαί as follows. Souls that fall under the same god choose a
life (αἱροῦνται βίον, p. 279, 15) that is either appropriate to
themselves or inappropriate. As Festugière explains,[17] a life is
appropriate to the soul insofar as that life displays the characteristics appropriate to the soul's leader god: "for example, if they
are ranked under the sun (Apollo), they normally propose for them-

selves a solar life." But some souls have enjoyment of the same

god according to different powers. Proclus writes (p. 279, 17-20):

> But what about the following: if souls dependent on the
> mantic power of the sun should project (προβάλλοιντο)
> a medical or telestic life, but other souls project a
> mercurial or lunar life? For the manner of variation
> is not the same for both.

The meaning of λόγων προβολαί now becomes evident. This

so called "projection of λόγοι" is actually a particular kind of
[18]
life that the soul puts forward from itself.   It is clear from

Proclus' account that the soul itself chooses the life that it will

project (αἱροῦνται βίον, p. 279, 15). Now, a soul can choose a life

appropriate to its leader god or not, and once that choice is made,

it can also project a life that is somehow in harmony with that god

or one that varies from him. Thus, a life that is appropriate to

the sun is a solar life, but a solar life can be of different kinds:

medical, telestic, etc. If a soul projects one of these lives, its

life corresponds to its god. However, a soul, while partaking of

the power of its leader-god, can also project a life that is appropriate

to another god.

This, then, is the explanation of Proclus' λόγων προβολαί

There is some evidence that suggests that Proclus is elaborating

upon Iamblichean doctrine. First, Iamblichus believed that the

gods had different powers. The terms "medical" (ἰατρικόν) and

"telestic" (τελεστικόν)[19] used by Proclus appear earlier in the

Timaeus (24c1). There they describe two types of arts given to

humanity by Athena. Iamblichus, in his commentary on this passage

(In Tim. Fr. 19) takes the two traits as solar. The "medical"

power of the sun seems to be connected with Asclepius, the "telestic"

power with Apollo.[20] Thus, it seems that Iamblichus, like Proclus,
divided the sun's power into different parts.

Second, there is reason to believe that the λόγων προβολαί
is Iamblichean. In De Myst. I 8, Iamblichus argues against Porphyry's
view that gods, demons, and souls are differentiated by their bodies:
the gods having ethereal bodies, demons aerial bodies, and souls
earthly bodies. After arguing that the greater kinds transcend
bodies, Iamblichus turns to the human soul (p. 25, 7-12):

> For such is the life (βίον) that the soul projected
> (προὔβαλε) before it entered the human body and such
> the form (εἶδος) it made ready for itself, so also is
> the organic body it holds united to itself and the similar
> nature following along with the body, [a nature] which
> receives the soul's more perfect life (ζωήν).

There are two points of similarity between Proclus' and
Iamblichus' theories. First, both concern a soul's choice (or
"projection") of a life before the soul enters its body. Second,
Iamblichus' discussion, like Proclus', is connected with a larger
argument about the connection between the greater kinds and the
human soul. Iamblichus stresses the dependence of the lower
entities upon the higher ones (p. 26, 6-14). Thus, a human soul's
projection of a particular form of life determines the nature of
the body that will eventually accept it. The soul-in-body is
further removed from the greater kinds but is still connected to
them.

Of course, much is left unsaid in the passage from the
De Mysteriis. Nothing is said of the life the soul projects. It
is unknown whether Iamblichus divided such a life according to the
powers of the celestial gods. There is no explicit discussion of
the differences between the kinds of lives the different human

souls project. It is, therefore, difficult to determine how much
of Proclus' theory is Iamblichean. Nevertheless, it seems safe to
say that Iamblichus did believe in a connection between gods and
humanity through the greater kinds, that he did accept the sowing of
the souls into the visible gods, that he conceived of these gods
as having different powers, and that he proposed, at some level,
the projection of a life in a human body by each soul.

There is one other reason for believing that Iamblichus'
discussion in De Myst. I 8 forms part of the basis for Proclus'
λόγων προβολαί. The discussion of both philosophers is similar to
the choice of lives discussed by Plato in the myth of Er (Rep.
X.617d1-621b7). Plato describes several souls choosing the lives
that they will lead on earth (ἕκασται αἱ ψυχαὶ ᾑροῦντο τοὺς
βίους, 619e6-620a1). Plato's myth concerns the choice made by souls
in Hades before they re-enter human bodies instead of the first
such entry discussed by Iamblichus and Proclus. Of course, Plato
does not mention the demiurgic sowing nor does he use the word
προβάλλειν, these being later neoplatonic interpretations. Nonetheless, it is clear that the neoplatonic concept of a soul choosing a
human life derives from this passage. It seems probable, therefore,
that Iamblichus developed his theory of a soul's projection of its
life from this myth and connected it with the Timaeus' creation
myth. If this is the case, Proclus would have adopted Iamblichus'
interpretation and elaborated upon it.

Proclus' third difference between souls is κατὰ τὰς
προαιρέσεις (p. 279, 20-21). A soul, Proclus says, even if it
chooses a telestic life, can still live that life either rightly

or distortedly. The final difference, then, preserves the soul's free will and allows the soul the choice of living its life well or badly. There is nothing here with which Iamblichus would disagree,[21] but whether or not he used the argument at this point in his Timaeus commentary is impossible to know.

Thus, there appears to be some agreement between Iamblichus and Proclus with regard to the differences between souls even though Iamblichus himself sees the sowing as a feature making all souls equal (that is, not slighted by the Demiurge, Tim. 41e3) by giving each its own leader god. Iamblichus' and Proclus' view about what the sowing entails is also similar, although Proclus' is more elaborate.

The second passage of the Timaeus in which the sowing is mentioned occurs at 42d4-5. Here the sowing is explicitly said to occur into the earth, moon, and other organs of time. Proclus (In Tim. III, pp. 304, 30-305, 11) considers the role of this sowing. First, the sowing occurs around the "young gods," i.e., around the cosmic gods. Proclus understands this sowing as involving the soul together with its vehicle. The soul and its vehicle are arranged under the circulations of the celestial gods. The sowing effects a twofold connection of human souls and the gods: the soul's power (δύναμις, p. 305, 7) is encompassed by the god's soul and the soul's vehicle is filled by the god's vehicle with the god's personal nature (ἰδιότης, line 10). Thus, the human soul is conjoined to the god's soul and the soul's vehicle to the god's vehicle. Again, there is nothing here with which Iamblichus would disagree.[22]

Proclus continues (p. 305, 11-26) by arguing that souls

are not sown into the Soul of the Universe. Iamblichus would agree
with this argument. In <u>De An</u>. I, p. 377, 16-19, Iamblichus mentions
only the greater kinds, heaven, and the elements as places into which
the demiurgic sowing occurs. Later, in line 23, when he does say
that the Universal Soul receives the whole cosmos as its place or
allotment, he does not mean that souls are sown into the Universal
Soul but only that the Universal Soul itself is allotted the cosmos
in the progression (πρόοδος, line 22) of souls.

Next Proclus (p. 305, 26-30) states that the sowing also
occurs "in each element (στοιχεῖον) under the moon." Iamblichus,
too, had included the elements in the sowing: εἰς ὅλα τὰ στοιχεῖα
τοῦ παντός (<u>De An</u>. I, p. 377, 19). Festugière (216-217 n. 5),
however, argues that the word στοιχεῖα here means "planets."
Festugière goes on to say that when Iamblichus uses the same word
(στοιχεῖον, lines 24-25) five lines later, it means not "planets"
but "the four regions of the world that are divided, from high
to low, into the four elements."

It would be most strange if Iamblichus were to use the
same word in two radically different senses in such a short space
of time. However, Proclus has made the meaning of Iamblichus' use
of the word clear by adding ὑπὸ σελήνην to στοιχεῖον in his own
commentary (p. 305, 26-27). The first occurrence of στοιχεῖον in
Iamblichus' <u>De Anima</u> passage does not refer to the planets but to
the sublunar regions or bands of elements. Therefore, when Iamblichus
says that the Demiurge sows souls "into all the elements of the
universe," he means that the sowing occurs under the moon.

This sowing into the elements under the moon does not
refer, as one might first suspect, to the sowing into the greater

kinds in line 18. Rather, since the sowing is of souls and vehicles
into the souls and vehicles of some deity, the elements here refer
to the sublunar gods. For Proclus, the sublunar gods are mentioned
by Plato at Tim. 41a4: "the gods who appear as they will." As
Dillon (368-369) points out, this identification is probably
Iamblichean. Furthermore, in In Tim. Fr. 77, Iamblichus specifically
arranges the sublunar gods Phorcys, Cronos, and Rhea "over the three
spheres between the earth and heaven." Iamblichus thinks that:[23]

> Phorcys . . . rules over the whole moist substance,
> holding it all together without division (ἀμερίστως
> συνέχων). Rhea is the goddess who holds together
> the fluid and aery influences (ῥεόντων . . . καὶ
> ἀεροειδῶν πνευμάτων). Cronos sets in order the
> highest and most rarified area of the aether.

Thus Iamblichus envisions three sublunary gods presiding over three
of the elements under the moon: Phorcys over water, Rhea over air,
and Cronos over ether.[24] It is for such deities as these that
Iamblichus uses the term στοιχεῖα, not for the planets, which are
above the moon.

Proclus next considers the upper limit of the sowing, that
is, whether or not souls are sown into the fixed stars (pp. 306,
13-307, 26). Iamblichus does not specifically mention the stars in
the passage from the De Anima, but he does say that the sowing occurs
καθ' ὅλον δὲ τὸν οὐρανόν (p. 377, 18-19), a phrase that keeps open
the possibility that the souls are sown around the stars. Again
the evidence for Iamblichus' view is sketchy, but there is some
reason for believing that he, like Proclus, thought that souls
were sown into the stars.

Proclus' argument turns upon a distinction between the
sowing and the distribution (νομή). It is clear from In Tim. III,

p. 307, 28-29 that the doctrine of the distribution is based upon
Tim. 41d8-e1: "Having organized τὸ πᾶν, he [i.e., the Demiurge]
divided the souls equal in number to the stars, and he distributed
(ἔνειμεν) each soul to each star." The neoplatonic doctrine of the
distribution of souls derives from the verb νέμειν here.

Iamblichus, in the De Anima passage, does not use the term
"distribution." However, in the next paragraph (p. 378, 1-18),
in which he discusses the views of other Platonists, the term appears
in the plural (νομάς, line 4). Iamblichus says that these Platonists
deny that the descents of the soul are involved with either the
demiurgic allotments, or the divisions among the greater kinds, or
the distributions (νομάς) in the universe.

There is a hierarchy expressed in this passage that suggests
that Iamblichus' use of the word νομάς refers to the neoplatonic
doctrine of the distribution of souls. The phrase "demiurgic
allotments" (δημιουργικοὺς κλήρους, p. 378, 2) refers to the soul's
λῆξις discussed on p. 377, 25-28. For Iamblichus, each soul is
assigned an allotment along with the sowing. The divisions
(διαιρέσεις, p. 378, 2) among the greater kinds refer directly to
the sowing itself: δημιουργὸν διασπείροντα περὶ πάντα μὲν τὰ
κρείττονα γένη, p. 377, 17-18. The word διαιρέσεις comes from the
participle διαιρουμένη, p. 377, 20-21. Thus, the hierarchy is
given in ascending order: these Platonists deny the soul's allotment,
sowing, and distribution. Seen in this way, the νομὴ τοῦ
παντός is prior to the sowing itself and, therefore, equivalent to
the distribution of souls to stars discussed by Proclus.

Indeed, Iamblichus' argument against the Platonists

appears to be directed against their refusal to accept the soul's placement into the souls and vehicles of the gods and other greater kinds. Iamblichus represents these Platonists as positing that the human soul is always in a body and that it enters from more subtle (λεπτότερα) bodies into more dense (ὀστρεῶδη) ones (p. 378, 6-8). Such a view is similar to Iamblichus' own doctrine of the vehicle. The problem, as Iamblichus would see it, is not with this doctrine. Rather, these Platonists err in not seeing that the human soul is connected to the souls of the greater kinds, the soul's vehicle to the vehicles of the greater kinds. But this connection is brought about through the distribution of the soul and through the sowing of the vehicle, two doctrines that these Platonists do not accept.

Proclus' commentary (In Tim. III, pp. 260, 7-265, 12) gives the standard neoplatonic interpretation of the distribution. Proclus begins (p. 260, 7-26) by summarizing the Iamblichean doctrine that the different classes of soul are ranked in order, the more partial under the more universal. Since the divine souls were already created by this point in the Timaeus, the souls to be distributed are the more partial souls. Proclus says that Plato will later (Tim. 41e1-2) have the Demiurge "arrange their vehicles under the divine circulations" (p. 260, 19-20). For now, however, the souls are not yet encosmic and are apportioned to the starry gods (lines 24-25). For, Proclus says (lines 25-26), the word "stars" here refers to "the souls of the starry bodies."

Throughout his discussion, as throughout this whole section,[25] Proclus does not mention the views of any other neoplatonic philosopher. It is impossible, therefore, to say how much Proclus is following Iamblichus or Syrianus and how much is his own. Nevertheless,

Iamblichus must have had some thoughts about this passage from
the Timaeus, and it is probable that they would have been similar
to Proclus'.

This assertion becomes more probable when one considers the
context of Tim. 41d8-e1. In Tim. 41a3-5, the visible gods (both
above and below the moon) have been created. Next (41a7-d3), the
Demiurge addresses these gods and orders them to create the three
remaining mortal creatures (which, for Iamblichus, are the greater kinds
and human beings). In this speech, the Demiurge makes it clear that
he will provide some part of these creatures (namely, for the neoplatonists, the immortal part)[26] and the young gods will provide the
rest and "weave mortal to immortal" (41d1-2). After this speech, the
Demiurge turns to the mixing bowl and blends the other, inferior souls
(41d4-8).[27] It is at this point that the present passage occurs.
The Demiurge organizes τὸ πᾶν, i.e., the total multitude of inferior
souls[28] and distributes them among the stars. Finally, at 41e1-2,
the Demiurge sets the souls upon vehicles.

Thus, for a neoplatonist like Iamblichus, the so-called
"distribution" of souls among the stars must take place prior to
the sowing of the soul together with its vehicle because the soul
has not yet been attached to its vehicle. Thus, once this sequence
of events is admitted, it is hard to imagine Iamblichus' description
of the distribution differing radically from Proclus'.[29]

Once it is admitted that Proclus and Iamblichus held similar
opinions concerning the distribution, it follows that for both
philosophers the differentiating feature between the sowing and the
distribution is not the level at which they occur (that is, that

the distribution occurs into the stars and the sowing into the planets) but the fact that the distribution unites the human soul to the god's soul and the sowing connects the human's vehicle to the god's vehicle. This argument is made forcefully by Proclus at In Tim. III, pp. 307, 26-308, 7) by arguing from Plato's own words that what is sown and what is distributed are different. In Tim. 41e1, Plato uses the feminine pronoun (ἑκάστην) when he says that "each is distributed into each" star, but in Tim 42d4-5, Plato uses the masculine definite article (τούς) when he says that the Demiurge "sowed some into the earth, others into the moon, and others into the other organs of time." For Proclus, the use of the feminine ἑκάστη indicates that it is the soul (ψυχή) that is being distributed, while the use of the masculine τούς shows that Plato had a human being, i.e., "a soul using a body" (p. 307, 31-32), in mind.[30]

Next (p. 308, 7-14), Proclus argues that both stars and planets have their own periodic returns (ἀποκαταστάσεις) and that the human ἀποκατάστασις is dependent upon that of its god. However, Proclus argues, if the human soul is distributed into a star but sown into a planet, the soul will have two different ἀποκαταστάσεις (both that of the star and that of the planet), but this is impossible. Therefore, every human soul is distributed and sown into the same god.[31]

Third (pp. 308, 14-309, 5), having argued that the distribution and sowing of any one soul occur into the same god, Proclus must show how Plato's words are to be interpreted. Proclus does so by arguing that the earth is a "star" insofar as it has an

"ethereal starlike vehicle" (p. 308, 16; cp. 309, 3) and that the
stars are "organs of time" in that they "help to complete time."[32]
Thus, Proclus concludes, when Plato says that the distribution is
into stars and the sowing into "the last of wholes, the moon and
the earth, he shows the worthiness of each, as the one [i.e., the
distribution] is more divine since it is incorporeal but the other
[i.e., the sowing] is inferior since the sowing is with bodies"
(p. 308, 28-32). Thus, for Proclus, a star has something "earthlike"
in it and the earth has something "starlike." Therefore, the distribution into "stars" refers not to the stars per se but to all the
celestial gods, and the sowing into the "organs of time" includes
not just the planets and other young gods but the stars as well.

The fourth section of Proclus' argument (p. 309, 16-20)
sums up what has been said and distinguishes between the distribution
and the sowing. The sowing is of bodies (i.e., of vehicles) but
the distribution is of incorporeals (i.e., of souls). The sowing
(being corporeal) involves the placing of the human vehicle into
those of the gods; the distribution (being incorporeal) is a mere
"separation in accordance with form" (κατ' εἶδος . . . διάκρισις, line
19). In other words, the distribution transcends the corporeal
sowing.

It is impossible to say if Iamblichus made all of the
four arguments above. Since, as has been argued, he accepted the
doctrines both of the distribution and the sowing, it is likely
that he would have said something about the difference between them.
Nevertheless, it remains an open question whether he delved as far
into the problem as Proclus did. Only the fourth argument of Proclus,

for the reasons given above in this section, can safely be called
Iamblichean.

Proclus summarizes his position at In Tim. p. 266, 11-14:

> For first they [i.e., human souls] come into existence
> (ὑπέστησαν), then they are distributed (διενεμήθησαν)
> around the divine rule (θείας ἡγεμονίας), and third
> they are mounted (ἐπέβησαν) on vehicles, view nature,
> and hear the fated laws.

Based on the arguments given in this section, it would
seem that Proclus and Iamblichus are pretty much in agreement about
this summary. The order is taken directly from the Timaeus (or,
at least, from a neoplatonic interpretation of that work). However,
there is one last passage from Proclus' commentary that sheds light
on an important difference between Iamblichus' and Proclus'
interpretation of Plato.

The passage in question (In Tim. III, pp. 233, 4-234, 5) is
a commentary on Tim. 41c6-d1:

> In as much as it is proper that they [i.e., the souls]
> have that which is of like kind with the immortals
> (ἀθανάτοις ὁμώνυμον), that which is called divine
> and which rules over those among them who always
> willingly follow justice and you [i.e., the young
> gods] , I [i.e., the Demiurge], having sown (σπείρας)
> and begun (ὑπαρξάμενος), will hand them over.

This Platonic passage appears in the Demiurge's speech to the
young gods. For a neoplatonist, the Demiurge is explaining that
he will create the immortal parts of the human soul. In order to
discover what it is that the Demiurge creates, Proclus focuses on
the words σπείρας and ὑπαρξάμενος.

The issue of the sowing is a complex one. Proclus discusses
three theories (p. 233, 4-22). First, there is the view of "many
of the Platonists" (line 5), according to which the sowing is the

"distribution (διανομήν) of souls around the stars." In order to
support this first view, Proclus cites Tim. 42d4-5 and says: "For
he [i.e., Plato] says 'he sowed some (τὰς μέν) into the earth,
some into the sun, and some into the moon.'" These Platonists,
therefore, thought that the sowing mentioned here was the same as
that mentioned at 42d.

The second view is unattributed. Proclus simply says
(p. 233, 8-10): "And will we posit a double sowing, one around the
gods and another around generation, the latter of which is given
in the Politicus?" The reference is to Plato's Politicus 272d6-
273a1. This passage occurs in the myth, told by the Eleatic
stranger to the young Socrates, concerning life on the earth in an
earlier time under the god Cronus. At this point in the myth, the
Eleatic stranger is discussing the end of that Saturnian age,
when "all the generations of every soul are yielded up and each soul
as a seed (σπέρμα) has fallen to the earth as often as was
arranged for it" (272e1-3). The sowing in the Proclus passage takes
its name from Plato's use of the word σπέρμα. For a neoplatonist,
then, this discussion of the close of the Saturnian age probably
represents the end of one cosmic era (ἀποκατάστασις), as the notion
of a certain number of births allotted to the human souls suggests.[33]
The "sowing" in the Politicus, however, is around generation (γένεσις,
272e2) and therefore differs from the Timaeus' sowing around the
divine circulations. Thus, the second view discussed by Proclus equates
the sowing of Tim. 41c8 not only with that mentioned in Tim. 42d4 but
also with that (supposedly) mentioned in Politicus 272e3. In other
words, the Demiurge is responsible for the sowing of souls both into
the celestial sphere and onto the earth itself.

Proclus himself disagrees with both views. He prefers
Syrianus' explanation, which makes a threefold division. The
sowing here refers to the generation (γένεσις, p. 233, 14) of the
soul. There are, then, three sowings: the one is actually the
Demiurge's generation of the soul, the second "the one around the
young gods" (p. 233, 18-19), and the third "the one around generation"
(p. 233, 19).

Proclus' discussion here (and probably throughout this
chapter of his commentary) is based upon Syrianus' lost commentary.
Syrianus' theory given here is typical of him, combining as it does
several points raised by previous philosophers.[34] Now, if the third
of Proclus' list of rival theories is Syrianus', it follows that
Iamblichus' view differed from both Syrianus' and Proclus'. This
raises the question whether either of the first two theories are
Iamblichus'.

There is good reason to believe that the second view
expounded by Proclus is Iamblichus'. The first theory is attributed
to "many of the Platonists." Earlier in this chapter (p. 231, 6)
Proclus also refers to certain Platonists. These Platonists, against
whom Proclus is arguing, claim that the human soul is "equal in
weight" (ἰσοστάσιος, lines 6-7) and "of the same substance"
(ὁμοούσιος, line 7) with divine souls. As Festugière[35] points out,
these Platonists are the same ones that Proclus calls νεώτεροι
at p. 245, 19-20. In that passage, the "more recent" philosophers
say that the human soul is "equal in worth" (ἰσάξιος, p. 245, 20)
and "of the same substance" (ὁμοούσιος, p. 245, 21) with divine
souls. By way of example,[36] Proclus mentions Plotinus (p. 245, 27)

and Theodorus (p. 246, 27). It is reasonable to assume, therefore, that the "many Platonists" mentioned at p. 233, 5 are again the "more recent" ones. However, Proclus' use of the verb διαθρυλοῦσι (p. 233, 5-6) signals a kind of contempt that is inappropriate for use against the divine Iamblichus. Rather, it seems the milder and almost acquiescent mention of the second view is more in harmony with Proclus' expressions of Iamblichus' theories. Indeed, Proclus does not dismiss the second theory at all but accepts it with certain qualifications, namely that there is a third sowing that Plato alludes to in the present passage,

Furthermore, once the second theory is attributed to Iamblichus, the series of the argumentation becomes clearer. Proclus, it has been suggested, is following an argument put forward by Syrianus. But what is Syrianus' source? It makes most sense to say that Syrianus is commenting upon an argument taken from Iamblichus' commentary. In other words, Iamblichus himself, in his discussion of Tim. 41c6-dl, raises the problem of what the sowing here refers to. After giving the standard interpretation of the "many Platonists," he goes on to correct them.

The hypothesis that Proclus is using Iamblichus' discussion second hand through Syrianus gains support from the earlier citation of the Platonists (p. 231, 5-10). For although there (as here on p. 233, 8-10) Iamblichus' name is not mentioned, it is nonetheless a Iamblichean doctrine that is being expressed. In De An. I, p. 365, 7-21, Iamblichus argues against those--such as Numenius, Plotinus, Amelius, and Porphyry, i.e., the νεώτεροι--who believe that the human soul is "of similar composition (ὁμοιομερής), the same (αὐτή),

and one" with the souls above it[37] and who place "the noetic cosmos,
the gods, demons, the Good, and all the kinds greater than the soul"
into the human soul. Proclus' statement of the Platonists' beliefs
is very similar to Iamblichus'. Proclus claims that the Platonists
say the human soul "is the same (αὐτόν) with Intellect, the noetic
itself, and Being itself" (In Tim. III, p. 231, 8-9). Proclus and
Syrianus, like Iamblichus before them, wish to keep the human soul
separate from the divine. It would seem, therefore, that they are
following Iamblichus' commentary here.

Just as there was reason to suspect that Proclus and
Syrianus were following Iamblichus' commentary in the early part of
their chapter, certain lexical similarities between the theory of
the "many Platonists" (In Tim. III, p. 233, 4-8) and Iamblichus'
De An. I, pp. 457, 22-458, 2 also point to a Iamblichean source in
the later part. In the De Anima passage, Iamblichus is discussing
the soul's reascent and eventual reward. While doing so, he mentions
the Platonic view set forth in the Timaeus:[38]

> In the way that the souls were sown (ἐσπάρησαν) differently
> by the Demiurge, some into the sun and others into the
> earth, in the same way Plato's Timaeus leads them up
> the road up (ἄνοδον), each soul not going beyond its own
> proper boundary in the demiurgic sowing (καταβολῆς).

There are two points in which this text is similar to Proclus' and
different from Plato's Tim 42d4-5. First, whereas Iamblichus
mentions the sun and earth as the places into which the Demiurge sows
the souls, Plato mentions the earth, the moon, and "other organs
of time." Therefore, when Proclus (p. 233, 7-8) mentions the earth,
sun, and moon, it is reasonable to suspect that his source used more
than a simple text of Plato—specifically, it used a text that

included reference to the sun. Second, whereas Proclus (p. 307,
12-20) emphasizes Plato's use of the masculine definite articles
τοὺς μέν . . . τοὺς δέ . . . τοὺς δέ in Tim. 42d4-5, Proclus here
uses feminine forms: τὰς μέν . . . τὰς δέ . . . τὰς δέ. Again,
one suspects the use of another source, and again the evidence
points to Iamblichus. In the passage from the De Anima, Iamblichus
uses the feminine pronouns: ἄλλαι μέν . . . ἄλλαι δέ (p. 457,
24).[39] Since this passage from the De Anima is based upon Iamblichus'
own commentary to the Timaeus, it is reasonable to assume that it is
this commentary upon which Proclus' arguments are based. Thus, it
seems that Proclus was using Iamblichean theories throughout this
chapter of his Timaeus commentary and that he found these theories
laid out in Syrianus' commentary.[40]

Before a discussion of the precise disagreement between
Proclus (and Syrianus) and Iamblichus, it will be helpful to consider
Proclus' discussion of Plato's use of the word ὑπαρξάμενος (Tim.
41c8). Proclus (In Tim. III, pp. 233, 23-234, 5) interprets the
Demiurge's "beginning" in two ways. First, the Demiurge "begins"
since there are other causes that together with the Demiurge generate
(συναπογεννᾷ, p. 233, 24) the soul. As an example of another cause,
Proclus gives the ζωογονική. Since Iamblichus believes that the
Timaeus' mixing bowl is a ζωόγονος αἰτία (In Tim. Fr. 82) and since
the Demiurge uses the mixing bowl to generate the soul (Tim. 41d4-7),
it is clear that Iamblichus would agree with Proclus' first assertion.

Second, the Demiurge "himself generates the vehicle of
the soul and every life (ζωήν) in it, to which life the young gods
weave the mortal form of life" (In Tim. III, p. 233, 26-28). Thus

Proclus connects the "beginning" with the Demiurge's generation of
the vehicle and of the other lives in it, viz., the irrational lives,
which were discussed in section I above. Here, however, there is a
significant difference between Iamblichus' and Proclus' theories.
Proclus believes in two vehicles: the first is made up of the
summits (ἀκρότητες) of the irrational life, is created by the Demiurge
himself, and is eternal (pp. 236, 29-237, 1); the second is mortal
and woven to the first by the young gods (p. 237, 2-6).[41] Iamblichus,
of course, believed that the vehicle was single and immortal. Thus,
the "beginning" that the Demiurge makes refers to the vehicle itself.
What, then, does Iamblichus believe is woven (προσυφαίνοντες, Tim.
41d1-2) by the younger gods? An answer can be found in Proclus'
next chapter (pp. 234, 7-238, 26).

Proclus (p. 236, 6-31) gives three interpretations of the
word θνητόν (Tim. 42d1) before giving Syrianus' view, with which he
himself agrees (pp. 236, 31-238, 26). As Festugière has noted,[42]
the first of these three opinions is Iamblichus'. According to
this opinion, the mortal life is so-called because it is "body-like"
(σωματοειδής) and is involved with the mortal (p. 236, 10-11).
This mortal life is "the life in the vehicle" (τὴν ἐν τῷ ὀχήματι
ζωήν, line 9) that is woven to the immortal part by the young gods
Thus, when Plato says (Tim. 42d1-2) that the young gods will "weave
the mortal to the immortal," Iamblichus interprets this statement to
mean that they will conjoin the vehicle and the irrational soul to
the rational soul. This view differs from Proclus', in which the
secondary mortal vehicle is woven to the primary immortal vehicle.

Proclus disagrees with Iamblichus' interpretation of θνητόν

as σωματοειδές (p. 236, 11-17). For Proclus, what the young gods create is not immortal. However, Proclus must admit that the irrational soul and second vehicle survive the death of the body and undergo punishment in Hades (pp. 236, 11-237, 9). Thus, just as Proclus believes that there are two vehicles, so too he believes that the irrational life of the soul is divided between these two vehicles. The summit (ἀκρότης) of the irrational nature is immortal and housed in the immortal vehicle; the irrational soul itself is mortal and housed in the mortal vehicle. Both the second vehicle and irrational soul are created mortal by the young gods. For Iamblichus, the case is simpler: the single, ethereal vehicle is created by the Demiurge and shaped by the lives and powers of the visible gods. The irrational soul is created by the visible gods. Both are immortal.

These differences having been noted, the differences between Iamblichus' and Proclus' views of the Demiurge's "sowing and beginning" can now be discussed. Proclus associates the sowing of Tim. 41c8 with the Demiurge's generation (γένεσις, p. 233, 14) of the rational soul and the beginning with the generation of the first vehicle. Iamblichus takes this sowing as double--one around the gods and one around generation--and the beginning as the generation of the (one) vehicle. The difference between these two interpretations is one of timing. The two sowings and the generation of the vehicle which Iamblichus accepts both occur later, after the Demiurge's speech is finished. For Proclus, however, the sowing and the beginning are immediate occurrences. There may be other later sowings, but

88

the generation of the rational soul occurs at this moment in the
Timaeus.[43] The generation of the vehicle is accomplished at this
point.

This difference reflects different interpretations of the
Timaeus. For Iamblichus, the human soul does not come into existence
until it is mixed in the mixing bowl (Tim. 41d4-7). Although the
ethereal substance of the vehicle has already been made, the actual
individual vehicle is not generated until the Demiurge embarks the
soul upon it (Tim. 41e1-2). Thus Iamblichus would not have seen a
need for a first vehicle created earlier nor for a second mortal vehicle
made by the young gods.

It is important to remember, however, that Iamblichus does
not disagree with Proclus' and Syrianus' claim that the soul and its
vehicle are generated by the Demiurge himself. Indeed, the very
acceptance of the πρώτη ὑπόστασις of the human soul (De An. I,
p. 377, 16-17) and of an ethereal vehicle show that Iamblichus
agreed fully. He would simply reply that this "sowing" is not the
πρώτη ὑπόστασις and that there is only one vehicle.

There is one last point about this sowing. The second
sowing that Iamblichus embraces, the one around generation, is,
strictly speaking, not a sowing at all. It is, rather, the descent
of the soul and its vehicle into the realm of generation. It is
equivalent to the term κάθοδος, which Iamblichus employs at De An.
I, p. 377, 26-27.

This long analysis of several passages from Proclus'
Timaeus commentary shows both similarities and differences between
Iamblichus' and Proclus' theories of the soul's generation and descent.

It should be obvious not only that the passage from Iamblichus'
De Anima (I, p. 377, 16-29) is indeed a summary of Iamblichus'
Timaeus commentary but also that it is a greatly truncated one.
The full meaning of the De Anima passage could not have been understood without the insights garnered from Proclus' commentary. It
is time, therefore, to return to that De Anima passage and to interpret
it in the light of this additional evidence.

Iamblichus begins, as has been stated, by distinguishing
between the soul's πρώτη ὑπόστασις and its sowing. These represent
the first two stages in a soul's life: the rational soul existing
qua soul and the soul together with its vehicle in the cosmic realm.

Iamblichus divides the process of sowing into three stages.
The soul is sown "around the greater kinds, throughout all heaven,
and into all the elements of the universe" (lines 17-19). As has
been seen, the sowing involves the soul with its vehicle being placed
into the circulations of the cosmic gods. Thus, Iamblichus understands the sowing as occurring into both the gods above the moon and
those below it. Moreover, the sowing also occurs into the greater
kinds. In other words, the sowing places the individual soul under
the care not only of some god but also of some archangels, angels,
heroes, demons, etc. that follow that god.[44]

Along with this sowing occurs "the first procession of souls"
(ἡ πρώτη τῶν ψυχῶν πρόοδος, lines 21-22), and this procession
"holds with itself the places receiving the souls" (lines 22-23).
Iamblichus is careful to say that the procession is not the sowing
but only exists along with it (συνυφισταμένη, line 22). This "first
procession" is that from the mixing bowl (Tim. 41d4-7). For, in In

Tim. Fr. 82, Iamblichus associates the procession (πρόοδος) from
the mixing bowl with each soul's rank: "for according as is their
rank [i.e., that of the gods, greater kinds, and humans] relative
to one another, such is the procession from the mixing bowl which
they are allotted, receiving thence the defining boundaries of
life."[45] In the De Anima as well, Iamblichus associates the procession
with a soul's rank, and a hierarchy is established (p. 377, 23-25):[46]
"The Whole Soul has the cosmos, the souls of the visible gods have the
heavenly spheres, and the souls of the elements have the elements
themselves." Thus, the procession exists together with the sowing in
that the soul gains its position in the universe relative to its rank,
which in turn is determined by its procession from the mixing bowl:
primary souls proceed first and are allotted the highest position,
intermediate souls proceed second and are allotted intermediate
positions, and human souls proceed last and receive the lowest positions.
The sowing of a human soul, then, exists along with and in proportion
to its procession from the mixing bowl.

Once the soul is sown, it exists (together with its vehicle)
in its cosmic allotment (λῆξιν, p. 377, 26). This allotment gives
the soul its leader-god and was considered the soul's "first genesis"
(In Tim. Fr. 85). The sowing has made the souls equal to one another
(Tim. 41e1-42a1).

From the places allotted to them in the sowing, the souls
make their descents into generation (De An. I, p. 377, 26-29). The
descent, therefore, differs from the sowing in that it brings the
soul into contact with matter and generation.[47] The πρώτη ὑπόστασις
(lines 16-17), "demiurgic sowing" (lines 17-18), and the "descent"

(lines 26-27) represent three distinct phases in the soul's life:
its rational life, its life in the vehicle, and its life in the
body.

Iamblichus, therefore, seems to have followed a standard
neoplatonic interpretation of the soul's descent. Although he did
differ from Proclus on specific issues, the overall conception of
the soul's generation, distribution/sowing, and descent is the same.
In the De Anima passage, Iamblichus chooses to emphasize what for
him are the most important phases in the soul's life. He also
chooses to emphasize the intermediary role of the greater kinds, as
well as the different ranks of the souls of the gods, greater kinds,
and human beings.

B. The Reasons for the Soul's Descent

A major problem for any Platonist concerns the motives for
the individual soul's descent. In this portion of section III,
Iamblichus' solution to this dilemma will be presented. This
solution will be found to depend upon other of his metaphysical
and religious doctrines discussed above, and again the greater kinds
will play a role.

For the neoplatonists, the problem of the motive for the
soul's descent is inherited from Plato himself. For, the myth of
the Phaedrus (248a1-249d2), on the one hand, records that the
individual souls follow the gods with difficulty. Because of the
unruliness of their horses, the souls have a hard time discerning
the Forms and gaining knowledge of them. Thus, through a fault in
the soul itself, the soul falls into generation and into the cycle
of births. The creation myth of the Timaeus, on the other hand, has

the Demiurge send the individual souls down to generation by
necessity.[48]

Plotinus faces this supposed contradiction squarely. In
Enn. IV.8.1.23-50, he quotes both from Plato's Phaedo, Republic, and
Phaedrus to show that Plato blamed the soul for its descent
(μεμψάμενος τὴν τῆς ψυχῆς ἄφιξιν πρὸς σῶμα, lines 40-41) and
from the Timaeus to show that the descent of the soul was necessary
for the completion (τὸ τέλεον, line 48) of the universe. Plotinus'
solution to the dilemma changed somewhat over time.[49] In IV.8.5,
Plotinus makes his first attempt to reconcile the two disparate
views.[50] He begins by stating that the voluntary descent is not
discordant with the involuntary (lines 1-8). For, Plotinus says
(lines 8-10), although every movement to an inferior existence is
involuntary, nonetheless that movement, caused by one's own impulse
(φορά), can be said to be brought about for punishment. But,
at the same time, the individual soul is acting by a law of nature
and is sent by god (lines 10-14). Nevertheless, in spite of this
quasi-involuntary descent, Plotinus still sees a double sin (διττὴ
ἁμαρτία, line 16) in the descent. The one sin is the soul's
reason for descending, the second the evils the soul performs once
it has descended. The punishment for the former is the descent
itself, for the latter continual rebirth.

In a later essay (IV.3.13),[51] Plotinus attempts to solve
the problem by arguing that the soul enters the body as if
spontaneously (οἷον αὐτομάτως, lines 7-8). The descent is
"biological" or "instinctive"[52] like the growing of horns or the
growth of a tree. As a result, Plotinus concludes (line 17),

souls "do not descend willingly nor are they sent." However, here too there still exists the underlying notion of the soul's sin. For, in IV.3.12.1-2, the cause for the descent resembles "a sin of narcissism,"[53] since the soul, seeing its image "as if in the mirror of Dionysus," rushes headlong (ὁρμηθεῖσα, line 2) to generation.

In an essay written near the end of his life (I.1.12),[54] Plotinus makes his last attempt at reconciling the two reasons for the soul's descent. Here Plotinus states that the soul's descent is merely an illumination of what is below it. For Plotinus, this illumination is not ἁμαρτία. (Plotinus compares the illumination by the higher human soul to a shadow being cast.) What does the illuminating is the highest phase of soul, the intuitive phase. What is illuminated is the irrational phase of the soul or the image, there is no ἁμαρτία. If, however, more than illumination occurs—if the middle, discursive phase of the soul (see II.9.2.5-10) associates itself with the image—then a descent into the realm of matter occurs and the discursive faculty becomes weighed down by matter. Nevertheless, even in this case, the higher, intuitive phase of soul does not descend. Thus, in this final attempt, Plotinus argues that there is no ἁμαρτία, at least as far as the highest phase of the soul is concerned, because the highest phase never descends.

The "tension" between the voluntary and the necessary descent in Plotinus' philosophy recurs even in this final passage.[55] Although he has freed the highest phase of the soul from any fault or error, the middle, discursive phase can still choose to associate itself with the image. The soul's descent still involves ἁμαρτία.

Plotinus' solutions are not without problems.[56] Nonetheless, his straightforward confrontation of the issue (admitting, as he does, that the problem originates from Plato's writings and must be resolved in accordance with them) and his systematic attempts to find a philosophical solution to the problem forced other neo-platonists to come to some decision of their own.[57]

It is clear that Iamblichus' attempt at a solution is based upon Plotinus' writings. Of course, Iamblichus must dismiss Plotinus' last attempt because, for Iamblichus, there is no part of the soul that does not descend (In Tim. Fr. 87). Iamblichus appeals directly to Plato's Phaedrus myth, where the charioteer sinks (δύνει) into generation. Since the soul descends in its entirety, Iamblichus must discover another solution to the dilemma. His attempt, given in the De Anima, follows the groundwork laid by Plotinus, but Iamblichus comes to a different conclusion.

Festugière (69-73) has already pointed out three passages of importance in the De Anima: p. 375, 5-18; pp. 378, 19-379, 10; and p. 380, 6-19; to these should be added p. 380, 19-29. However, Festugière's purpose in examining these passages is to uncover some important issues in the soul's descent in Gnostic theory. As a result, he does not consider Iamblichus' own philosophical position. Nevertheless, these four passages do provide the evidence necessary for understanding Iamblichus' solution.

The first passage from the De Anima occurs as a digression on a longer section (pp. 374, 21-375, 28) on the relationship between the rational and irrational powers of the soul.[58] This digression concerns the origin of evil in the soul. Iamblichus distinguishes two groups of philosophers. The first group (consisting of Plotinus, Empedocles, Heraclitus, the Gnostics, and Albinus) argues that the cause of the soul's descent (αἰτίας γιγνομένης τῶν καταγωγῶν ἐνεργημάτων, p. 375, 11) occurs prior to the descent itself. The second group (consisting of Numenius, Cronius, Harpocration, Plotinus, and Porphyry) is said to oppose the first (διιστσμένων πρὸς τούτους, p. 375, 12) and to posit in addition (προστιθέντων, p. 375, 13) things external to the soul as the cause of evil. For this second group, evil arises externally after the soul's descent (p. 375, 14-18): "Numenius and often Cronius posit that evil arises from matter, Harpocration from these human bodies themselves, and Plotinus and Porphyry most often from the irrational life."

As the word προστιθέντων suggests, the two groups are not diametrically opposed. The second group accepts the claims of the first but would add to them, and as Festugière (69-70) notes, Plotinus appears in both groups. But this is not to say that Iamblichus accepts both positions himself. There is no indication of Iamblichus' beliefs in this passage. He is simply setting forth two positions held by philosophers before him. In so doing, he is making a conscious distinction between the soul's first fall and its subsequent descents.

Iamblichus' choice of philosophers in the first group shows that he was aware of Plotinus' attempts to solve the problem of the soul's descent (p. 375, 5-11):

> According to Plotinus, the cause of the descending
> energies is the first otherness (τῆς πρώτης ἑτερότητος),
> according to Empedocles the flight from god (τῆς ἀπὸ τοῦ
> θεοῦ φυγῆς), according to Heraclitus the rest in change
> (τῆς ἐν τῷ μεταβάλλεσθαι ἀναπαύλης), according to the
> Gnostics a derangement or deviation, and according to
> Albinus the erroneous decision of the free will.

As Festugière has pointed out,[59] there are various similarities

between Iamblichus' and Plotinus' words. In particular, the phrase

"first otherness" derives from Enn. V.1.1.1-5: Why, Plotinus asks,

have souls forgotten the Father? "The source of their evil is

τόλμα, γένεσις, the first otherness (ἡ πρώτη ἑτερότης), and their

desire for independence." The references to Empedocles and Heraclitus

also come from the Enneads. In IV.8.1.11-23 and IV.8.5.5-8, Plotinus

mentions these two presocratics together, and again the phraseology

is similar to Iamblichus': for Empedocles, φυγὰς θεόθεν, 8.1.19

and φυγὴ ἀπὸ τοῦ θεοῦ, 8.5.5; for Heraclitus, μετάβαλλον ἀναπαύεται,

8.1.13-14 and ἀνάπαυλα ἐν τῇ φυγῇ, 8.5.6-7. Of course, it is still

possible that Iamblichus and Plotinus are quoting from a common source,

but given that Iamblichus has just quoted from (and is, therefore,

familiar with) Enn. V.1.1, there seems little reason to deny that

he took the Empedocles and Heraclitus quotations from Plotinus as

well.[60]

The second passage from the De Anima (pp. 378, 19-379, 10)

concerns the different modes (τρόπους, 378, 21) of descent for

different souls. The passage is divided into two sections (378, 21-

379, 6 and 379, 7-10), each of which is further subdivided into two

opposing sections by Iamblichus' use of μέν . . . δέ. Each larger

section gives a different division (ἄλλην . . . διαίρεσιν, 379, 7)

of the modes of descent.

In the first section (378, 21-379, 6), Iamblichus contrasts
the views of Heraclitus and Taurus. In order to understand the
nature of the contrast that Iamblichus makes, it will be necessary
to understand the different points of view attributed here to
Heraclitus and Taurus.

Of Heraclitus, Iamblichus says (378, 21-25):

> Heraclitus, on the one hand, posits that changes occur
> necessarily from opposites. He supposed that souls
> traveled the road up and down and that for these souls
> to remain is toil and to change brings rest.

This reference to Heraclitus, of course, recalls and amplifies the
earlier reference to him at p. 375, 7-8. There Heraclitus was included
with Plotinus, Empedocles, the Gnostics, and Albinus. All these
philosophers held that the cause of the soul's descent occurred prior
to that descent.

Festugière (71) has expressed astonishment that Iamblichus
mentions Heraclitus alone here when in the earlier passage Iamblichus
had mentioned him in connection with Plotinus and the rest. Festugière
cannot decide whether this omission occurs because Iamblichus had
sufficiently dealt with the other opinions earlier or whether "this
is, rather, a new proof of the superficial methods" of Iamblichus.
A closer examination will reveal a better reason.

In both passages (375, 5-11 and 378, 21-25), Iamblichus
is following Plotinus. If one looks at Plotinus' words concerning
the opinions of Heraclitus and of Empedocles, one will see that
Plotinus places the two philosophers in different camps. In
Enn. IV.8.1, Plotinus is considering the reason for the soul's
descent into the body. He gives the views of Heraclitus and
Empedocles (lines 11-15, 17-20):

> For Heraclitus, who orders us to seek for this [i.e.,
> the reason souls descend], posits that change is
> necessarily from opposites, mentions the road up and
> down, that "change rests" and "it is toil for the same
> things to labor and to be ruled" . . . And Empedocles
> says that it is a law for souls that err (ἁμαρτανούσαις)
> to fall here and that he himself was "a fugitive from god"
> and came here "having trusted in raving strife."

Here, just as in De An. I, p. 378, 21, Heraclitus is seen as

explaining the soul's descent as necessary (ἀναγκαίας, Enn. IV.8.

1.12). Empedocles, on the other hand, sees the cause for the soul's

descent as sin. The same point is made at Enn. IV.8.5.5-8. Here,

Empedocles' "flight or wandering from god" is equated with "the

error (ἁμαρτία) for which there is punishment" and contrasted with

Heraclitus' "rest in the flight." Again the notion of voluntary

fault contrasts with that of necessity.

For Plotinus, then, Heraclitus and Empedocles represent

two contrasting positions concerning the soul's descent. Empedocles'

doctrine emphasizes the soul's τόλμα Heraclitus' the necessity of

the descent. If Plotinus makes this distinction, it is natural

that Iamblichus, who is following him, would do so as well. Moreover,

it is clear from De An. I, p. 378, 21-25 that Iamblichus considers

Heraclitus' doctrine to involve necessity (ἀναγκαίας, line 22), and

Iamblichus certainly considers the doctrines of the other philosophers

mentioned at 375, 5-11 to involve a willful sin, as his words there

suggest.[61]

Iamblichus mentions only Heraclitus at 378, 21-25, therefore,

because he does not wish to discuss τόλμα as the reason for the

soul's descent. As will be argued below, Iamblichus rejects τόλμα

as a cause for the descent.

For Iamblichus, then, Heraclitus posits the belief that

all change comes about necessarily through opposites. This law

includes the ascents and descents of the soul (ὁδόν τε ἄνω καὶ

κάτω, 378, 23). The cause of the descent is some cosmic law that

the souls must follow.

After his discussion of Heraclitus (378, 21-25), Iamblichus

turns to the philosophy of Taurus and says (378, 25-379, 6):

> Those around Taurus, on the other hand, say that souls
> are sent to earth by the gods: some, who follow the
> Timaeus, teach that this occurs for the completion of
> the universe, so that there might be as many living
> things in the cosmos as there are in the noetic realm;
> others set up the goal of the descent as a demonstration
> of divine life. For, this is the will of the gods: to
> show themselves as gods through the souls. For, the
> gods come forth into the open and show themselves through
> the pure and immaculate life of souls.

The view of Taurus differs from Heraclitus' in emphasis.

The cosmic law is now attributed to the gods: πέμπεσθαι

τὰς ψυχὰς ὑπὸ θεῶν, 378, 26. Taurus gives two ways to account for

his theory: the explanation is either philosophical or religious.[62]

The first method, as Iamblichus says (378, 27), follows

Plato's Timaeus.[63] The soul descends for the completion (τελείωσιν,

378, 28) of the universe. Again there is no room for τόλμα in this

conception. The soul is sent down by the gods in order that there

will be as many kinds of living entities in this realm as there are

in the noetic realm.

Taurus' second method does not rest upon the word of Plato

but upon religious beliefs. The soul is sent by the gods so that

the gods may somehow display themselves through the souls. Neither

Festugière nor Dillon have been able to uncover any precedent for

such a belief.[64] It seems likely that this was Taurus' own addition.

It further appears that Iamblichus approved it. For, in explaining
Taurus' position, Iamblichus suddenly ceases to speak in indirect
statement (οἱ δὲ . . . ἀναφέροντες . . . εἶναι . . . ἐκφαίνεσθαι,
379, 1-4) and expresses a supporting argument in the present
indicative (379, 4-6): "For (γάρ) the gods come forth (προέρχονται)
into the open and show themselves (ἐπιδείκνυνται) through the pure
and immaculate life of souls."

It is not at all surprising that Iamblichus would endorse
Taurus' view. Taurus' second view is compatible with his first,
which was based upon Plato's doctrine in the Timaeus. It is a
special class of souls that Taurus is considering in the second case,
the class of pure and undefiled souls.[65] Thus, his religious reason
for the soul's descent is an addition to, not a contradiction of,
the explanation of the Timaeus: all souls are sent to the earth by
the gods, but the pure ones are sent not only to complete the universe
but also to display the gods through the souls' lives here. Moreover,
as even a casual reading of his philosophical works suggests,
Iamblichus is eager to seize upon religion as a support for his
views. He particularly enjoys showing that the Platonists (including
Plotinus and Porphyry) do not take the "ancients" (i.e., theurgists,
practitioners of the ancient religion) into account.[66] Therefore,
Iamblichus would have found Taurus' view refreshing and would have
hastened to approve it.

As was said above, the distinction between Heraclitus'
and Taurus' views is one of emphasis. Each gives a reason for the
descent that is external to the soul. The two views are not
necessarily incompatible. The Timaeus makes the descent

of the soul necessary, just as Heraclitus does (or, rather, as
the neoplatonic interpretation of Heraclitus' philosophy does).
It is more likely that Iamblichus is simply contrasting two ways
of viewing the same phenomenon.

Following the discussion of Heraclitus' and Taurus'
views, Iamblichus says (379, 7-10):

> According to another division, some modes of descent are
> thought to be voluntary (the soul either choosing the
> administration of things around the earth or obeying its
> superiors) and others involuntary (the soul being forcibly
> dragged to an inferior existence).

This second passage presents an alternative way of looking
at the soul's descent. The earlier passage (pp. 378, 21-379, 6)
allowed only for a soul's descent by cosmic or divine law. The
distinction there was between two ways of viewing the law that
requires souls to descend. The distinction here in the second
passage, however, is between the soul's own willingness or unwilling-
ness in the necessary descent. In other words, although there is
a cosmic law that requires a soul to descend, the soul itself may
either assent and descend voluntarily or resist and be forced to
descend. The two types of distinction that Iamblichus makes,
therefore, are compatible.

Thus far, Iamblichus has set forth the beliefs of other
philosophers. In the third passage (p. 380, 6-19), Iamblichus
gives his own opinion about the causes of the soul's descent.

> I think that since the goals (τέλη) are different, this
> fact makes the modes of the descent of souls different
> also. The soul descending for the preservation, purifi-
> cation, and perfection of the things here makes its
> descent pure (ἄχραντον). The soul turning itself
> toward bodies for the sake of exercising and correcting
> its own character is not completely impassive nor does
> it enjoy its own independence (ἀπόλυτος καθ' ἑαυτήν).

The soul descending for punishment and judgment seems somehow dragged and forced. Certain more recent ones--especially Cronius, Numenius, and Harpocration--do not make these distinctions, and not taking into account the differences, they conflate the embodiments of all souls and affirm that all embodiments are evil.

Iamblichus distinguishes three "modes" of descent based upon three "goals" or purposes for which the soul makes its descent. As Festugière (222 nn. 2-4) mentions, these three kinds of descent are similar to those that Iamblichus has discussed before. Specifically, the soul that descends ἐπὶ σωτηρίᾳ καὶ καθάρσει καὶ τελειότητι τῶν τῆδε (380, 8-9) is similar to the soul that (in Taurus' conception) descends both εἰς τελείωσιν τοῦ παντός (378, 28) and to reveal the gods διὰ τῶν ψυχῶν καθαρᾶς καὶ ἀχράντου ζωῆς (379, 5-6). Such a soul descends voluntarily (379, 7-9). On the other hand, the soul that descends ἐπὶ δίκῃ καὶ κρίσει (380, 12-13) makes an involuntary descent (379, 10). However, Iamblichus has added a new category in between these two: the soul that descends διὰ γυμνασίαν καὶ ἐπανόρθωσιν τῶν οἰκείων ἠθῶν (380, 10). The reason for this new category, as will be seen, reflects Iamblichus' own religious philosophy. Before considering this point, however, it will be necessary to consider the kinds of souls and descents that Iamblichus has in mind.

The first category of souls, Iamblichus says, makes a pure (ἄχραντον) descent. This concept of a "pure" descent (and, therefore, of a "pure" soul) first occurred in Taurus' second explanation of the soul's descent. Taurus, Iamblichus says, referred the goal (τέλος, 379, 2) of the descent to a demonstration of divine life. Thus, certain "pure" souls descend for this purpose.

Moreover, at 379, 22-25, in a passage concerning the relationship of souls to bodies, Iamblichus says of the human soul: "Pure (καθαραί) and perfect (τέλειαι) souls enter into bodies purely (καθαρῶς) without passions and without being deprived of intellect. Opposite souls enter oppositely." Thus, it is clear that Iamblichus differentiated between different kinds of souls: pure and impure. At 380, 7-9, he extends this concept of a pure soul to its descent. Pure souls, which descend for the benefit of this realm, make a pure descent.

The concept of a pure soul is, of course, a religious/ theurgic one. A pure soul is one purified of all stains and sin. Iamblichus considered such souls special, as In Phaed. Fr. 5 shows. There Iamblichus claims that some souls do not descend from the noetic realm. He explains this unorthodox view by saying that they can be said not to descend "by reason of the form of their life which creates a descent which does not involve generation and which never breaks its connexion with the higher realm."[67] In other words, pure souls make a special kind of descent (so special, it seems, that Iamblichus would deny that the term "descent" properly applies to it). They remain pure even in this realm by their special connection to the noetic. It is such souls as these that make a "pure" descent and help in the administration of things in this realm.[68]

The pure soul's continuous connection to the noetic realm is important. Because of this connection, the souls can enter the material realm without being contaminated by it. It is this connection that keeps pure souls pure and allows them to be of benefit to less fortunate souls in this lower realm.

As was said above, such a descent is voluntary according to Iamblichus' definition at 379, 7-9: the soul either chooses to administer things in this realm or obeys the gods and descends. A pure soul is faced with the necessity of its descent but, being pure, has the wisdom to discern that the descent is for it good and pure. Hence, it descends willingly in accordance with the cosmic laws.

At first glance, Iamblichus' conception of a descent that is both necessary and voluntary may seem identical to Plotinus' (ἔχει τὸ ἑκούσιον ἢ ἀνάγκη, Enn. IV.8.5.3-4).[69] There is, however, a difference. For Plotinus, the soul's free will involves sin (ἁμαρτία, Enn. IV.8.5.16-17). For Iamblichus, on the other hand, the descent for these pure souls is good and is in accordance with divine law.[70] There is no τόλμα.

With regard to this category of pure souls, it is worth noting Iamblichus' dismissal of the opinions of Cronius, Numenius, and Harpocration (380, 14-19). These three philosophers were mentioned above in the first passage from the De Anima concerning the soul's descent (375, 14-16). There Numenius and Cronius are said to claim that matter is the source of evil to the soul, and Harpocration that bodies themselves are the source. Iamblichus would agree with their assessment in general but (at 380, 14-19) takes exception to their view that all embodiments are evil. What these three philosophers fail to discern is that there are different kinds of human soul and that for some of these souls (viz., the pure ones) embodiment is a good. Thus, by his conception of pure souls and

their pure descents and embodiments, Iamblichus solves two problems
in the history of Platonic philosophy. First, he removes τόλμα
as the reason for a soul's descent; pure souls descend voluntarily
but without sin. Second, he circumvents the movement toward
dualism (inherent in Gnosticism) by showing that embodiments are
not necessarily evil and that pure souls can live in this realm
yet remain pure.

Iamblichus' third category (380, 12-14) concerns those
souls that descend for punishment and judgment. As Festugière
(78-80) notes, the notion of the soul undergoing punishment and
judgment for sins committed in a previous life derives from the myth
of the Phaedrus (246d6-249d3). According to the myth (249a5-b1),
the souls

> whenever they have completed their first [earthly] life
> undergo judgment (κρίσις) and having been judged some
> come into places of punishment (δικαιωτήρια) and are
> punished (δίκην ἐκτίνουσιν) and others are lifted up
> by Justice to some heavenly place and live worthily
> according to the form of human life they had lived.

Souls are judged according to their lives on earth. Souls that
have sinned undergo judgment and punishment. Afterwards, according
to Plato (Phdr. 249b1-3), the souls choose their second life.

Iamblichus believes--along with Plotinus, Enn. IV.8.5.
16-20--that part of the punishment for the souls' past sins is to
descend again and to be reincarnated. These impure souls, like pure
souls, follow necessity,[71] but unlike them, descend against their
will (συρομένη πως ἔοικε καὶ συνελαυνομένη, 380, 13-14).[72]

Between these two categories there is another: souls that
descend to train and correct their characters (380, 9-12). These
souls are characterized as neither completely impassive nor as

completely independent. Thus, they are neither completely pure
nor completely impure but somewhere in between. As Festugière
(222 n. 3) points out, this is a new category, not corresponding
to any of those previously mentioned by Iamblichus. However, it
is a category completely consistent with Heraclitus' and Taurus'
view of the necessity of the descent, with the view of the descent
as voluntary, and with Plato's Phaedrus myth.

First, in the passage from the Phaedrus myth quoted above,
Plato distinguishes between souls that are punished and those that
live in heaven as worthily as their previous existence on earth
would allow. These latter souls are not completely impure and, hence,
are not sent to Hades for punishment.[73] Thus, Iamblichus seems to
conclude, these souls descend again and are given the opportunity to
better themselves.[74] Iamblichus probably had in mind initiates to
the sacred mysteries who were preparing for absolute purification
but needed more time and practice to become fully pure.[75]

Second, it must have been obvious to Iamblichus that if
there was a cosmic law that every soul must descend, then these
quasi-purified souls must descend as well. And if they descend in
order to perfect themselves, the descent must be voluntary in the
sense that they are obeying the gods who sent them. Again, the
descent is good and there is no τόλμα.

Iamblichus' solution to the problem of the soul's descent
answers the problems raised by Plotinus. For Iamblichus, the descent
occurs by necessity but the free will of the better souls is main-
tained. However, there is one problem that Iamblichus has not yet
addressed: if there is no τόλμα, why do souls first descend? In

other words, Iamblichus' solution makes sense as far as a soul

that has already lived on earth is concerned. After such a

life, the soul is either pure or in need of punishment or further

purification. But what of all these souls before their first

descent?

Iamblichus sets out to answer this question in the fourth

and final passage concerning the soul's descent (380, 19-29):

> It is necessary to know also the lives of souls before
> they enter into the body, since these lives hold great
> differences in themselves. From different kinds of life,
> the souls make for themselves their first encounter with
> bodies differently. For those newly initiated and who
> have seen much of true being (νεοτελεῖς καὶ πολυθεάμονες
> τῶν ὄντων), those accompanying and akin to the gods
> (συνοπαδοὶ καὶ συγγενεῖς τῶν θεῶν), and those perfect
> ones embracing the whole forms of the soul are without
> passions or defilement first implanted into bodies.
> But for those completely filled with desires and full
> of passions, it is with passions that they first
> encounter bodies.

Festugière (223 n. 1) has already indicated the parallels

between Iamblichus' vocabulary here and that of Plato in the Phaedrus

myth. Festugière (223 n. 2) has also noted that this passage concerns

the soul's existence before its first descent. It follows, therefore,

that Iamblichus thinks that the reason for the first descent and for

the subsequent division of souls into pure and impure souls is to

be found in Plato's Phaedrus myth.

According to the Phaedrus myth, the human souls with their

vehicles (called ὀχήματα at 247b2) and two horses follows their god

as best they can. The soul that handles itself best is carried around

the heavens with its god, raises its charioteer's head into heaven,

and attempts to contemplate the true beings there. A soul that is

successful is called θεῷ συνοπαδός (248c2) and is free from pain

for a complete thousand-year cycle (μέχρι τε τῆς ἑτέρας περιόδου
εἶναι ἀπήμονα, 248c4). An unsuccessful soul sheds its wings and falls
to earth.

Festugière (78) believes that in the Phaedrus, "Plato admits
to the notion of an original sin committed in heaven before the
descent and from which the descent results." Thus, if Iamblichus
were to accept the notion of τόλμα one would expect to find him
embracing it here. He clearly does not. The soul's fault lies not
in some willful act of disobedience but in the soul's inability to
control its recalcitrant horse (or passions). Festugière (78 n. 2)
thinks that the doctrine of the Phaedrus

> contrasts with that of the Timaeus, according to which,
> in the state in which they leave from the hands of God,
> the souls are all equally good, "and the first birth is
> established identical for all (human) beings in order
> that none might be treated less well by God" (Tim.
> 41e3-5). The inequalities only come afterwards, in the
> course of reincarnation.

There is, however, no such contrast in Iamblichus' mind. The
Timaeus passage cited by Festugière was discussed in section IIIA,
above. There is was seen that Iamblichus interpreted this "first
birth" (γένεσις πρώτη) as the demiurgic sowing of the human soul and
its vehicle into the circulation of its leader-god. Thus, the
equality that all souls share is a first celestial life under the
protection of some deity. The conception of the Phaedrus is, for
Iamblichus, no different. Here too the human soul and its vehicle
are placed into the circulation (περιφορά, Phdr. 248a4) of its
leader-god (θεὸς ἄρχων, Phdr. 247a3). Although each soul is
granted this celestial position, not every soul can keep to it.
The problems inherent in the irrational soul (the uncontrollable

horse) can prevent the soul from partaking fully of true being and,

thus, from being fully purified from passions.

    Two fragments from Iamblichus' Phaedrus commentary help

to show how Iamblichus interpreted the Phaedrus myth consistently

with the creation myth of the Timaeus. In In Phdr. Fr. 3,

Iamblichus equates Zeus in the Phaedrus myth (246e4) with the

Demiurge of the Timaeus, and the heaven (to which the Demiurge-Zeus

leads the other gods and demons) with the noetic realm. Thus, the

Demiurge is the great leader of all the celestial gods and demons

(by which latter term Iamblichus would have understood all the

greater kinds). The entourage of gods and greater kinds, therefore,

are led upward together to the noetic realm in which true being

resides.[76] It is clear from In Tim. Fr. 34 that the Demiurge is

a noetic entity. He is said to collect into one and hold in himself

(ἐν ἑνὶ συλλαβὼν ὑφ' ἑαυτὸν ἔχει) the entire noetic realm.[77]

Thus, it is only proper for Iamblichus to think that in the Phaedrus

the Demiurge leads the entourage of gods and greater kinds to his

own realm.

    In Phdr. Fr. 5 further confirms Iamblichus' belief in

the similarity between the two dialogs:[78]

> The great Iamblichus, having declared the great heaven
> to be an order of intelligible (νοητῶν) gods, which he
> has in some places identified with the Demiurge, takes
> the "inner vault of heaven" (ὑπουράνιον ἁψῖδα) as
> the order of creation situated immediately beneath it
> and as it were the membrane (ὑπεζωκυῖαν) covering
> heaven.

The phrase ὑπουράνιον ἁψῖδα occurs at Phdr. 247b1. There

Plato states that when the gods and their divine followers go to

feast (Phdr. 247a8-b2):

> they travel up to the high heavenly vault, where the
> gods' vehicles, being obedient to the rein, travel
> easily and well-balanced but the others with difficulty.
> For, the horse having a share of evil weighs it down.

Plato had already explained (246d6-e4) that the soul's wings are
nourished by the καλὸν, σοφὸν, ἀγαθὸν, καὶ πᾶν ὅτι τοιοῦτον
found in the noetic realm. Thus, the gods and their followers
nourish their wings by following the Demiurge-Zeus to the heavenly
vault, which Iamblichus equates with the upper boundary of the noeric
realm. It follows that the celestial gods, greater kinds, and human
souls (each in its vehicle) ascend no further than the highest point
in the noeric realm. More will be said about this in section IV,
below. For now all that need be noted is the harmony between
Iamblichus' conception of the metaphysical hierarchies of the
Phaedrus and Timaeus.[79]

For Iamblichus, then, the soul's first encounter with a
body is made purely and without passions if the soul is able to follow
its leader-god and glimpse the true beings of the noetic realm
before its embodiment. The encounter is made impurely if the soul
fails in its endeavor to follow. The soul that fails does so because,
try as it might, it cannot control its irrational nature. In
accordance with a cosmic law, both types of soul must fall and be
born. For Iamblichus, there is no contradiction between the fall
described in the Phaedrus and the cosmic law of the Timaeus.

It has been argued that Iamblichus squarely confronts
Plotinus' statement of the seeming contradiction between the reasons
for the descent given in Plato's Phaedrus and Timaeus. Iamblichus
believes that different classes of human souls descend for different

reasons but none descends because of willful audacity on the soul's part. There are several reasons for Iamblichus' rejection of the doctrine of the soul's τόλμα. First, of course, is the question of Plato's consistency. For any neoplatonist, the arguments of Plato in one dialog must be in harmony with those of another. Thus, Iamblichus harmonizes the theory of the soul's descent by arguing that all descents occur by necessity, whether or not the individual soul is willing to descend.

Second, all souls before the first descent are equal in purity. (The "first birth" or sowing assures this equality, according to Iamblichus' interpretation of Tim. 41e3-4.) All human souls are given an equal chance to follow their leader-gods and to remain pure. Those who succeed willingly make a pure descent in accordance with the divine law. Those who fail to follow their leader-god descend unwillingly but necessarily according to the same law. In neither case is the cause ascribed to a willful or audacious desire.

Furthermore, for Iamblichus especially, there is another reason to reject τόλμα as the cause of the first descent. He believes that not only human souls but also those of the greater kinds descend. It will be recalled that Iamblichus placed the greater kinds in the third hypothesis of Plato's Parmenides and that this placement was most unusual (In Parm. Fr. 2).[80] The reason for placing the greater kinds in their own Platonic hypothesis is, as has been seen, Iamblichus' insistence on the difference between the different classes of soul. In In Parm. Fr. 12, it can be seen that Iamblichus also relied upon the intermediary role of demons in Plato's

Symposium.[81] Clearly, Iamblichus accepted these demons and other
greater kinds as intermediaries between gods and humans. As such,
in accordance with the Symposium, they were neither divine nor human
themselves, but something in between. Therefore, in Iamblichus'
opinion, they deserved their own hypothesis.

The problem with placing the greater kinds in the third
hypothesis concerns the neoplatonic interpretation of Parm. 155e10:
"For at one time it [i.e., the subject of the third hypothesis]
participates and at another it does not." For other neoplatonists,
this sentence referred to the human soul, which sometimes participates
in the entities above (i.e., it ascends and is in contact with the
noetic realm) and sometimes does not (i.e., it descends and associates
with matter). Iamblichus, however, taking his metaphysical hierarchy
seriously, believes that the greater kinds undergo such ascents
and descents (In Parm. Fr. 13). The notion of any of the greater
kinds descending because they commit a willful sin against the gods
would be anathema to Iamblichus. Their souls, being mixed in the
mixing bowl second after the gods, are nearly divine and much purer
than any human soul. The reason for their descent, therefore, would
be similar to that for pure human souls: to help administer the
universe, in particular to act as intermediaries between gods and
humans. Their descents are pure; no τόλμα is involved.[82]

The above three reasons--the consistency of Plato's writings,
the purity of the soul in its pre-embodied state, and the need for
greater kinds to descend--do not fully explain Iamblichus' rejection
of τόλμα. He could have argued that there is some class of human
souls that does sin. A comparison of Iamblichus' philosophy with

Plotinus' shows another reason for Iamblichus' stance. For Plotinus,

the human soul contains within itself the ability to gain salvation.

Contemplation (θεωρία) is sufficient to withstand magic and popular

religion.[83] Just as the soul is free to save itself by its own

will, so too it is free to enslave itself by choosing to descend

into association with the body. For Iamblichus, on the other hand,

it is theurgy and not contemplation that brings human salvation

(De Myst. II 11, pp. 96, 13-97, 11):

> For it is not thinking (ἔννοια) that unites theurgists
> to the gods. Or what hinders those philosophizing by
> contemplation (θεωρητικῶς) from having theurgic union
> with the gods? But such is not the case. Rather, the
> efficacy of ineffable acts accomplished divinely
> (θεοπρεπῶς) beyond all intellection and the power of
> unspeakable symbols understood only by the gods impart
> theurgic union.

Theoretic philosophy is secondary to theurgic ritual. The human soul

cannot save itself but requires the help of the gods. So too, the

human soul in its pre-embodied state, under the protection of its

leader-god, does not itself choose to reject the gods and descend.

Throughout the entire cycle of a soul's existence, the human soul

is in the hands of the gods. It is sent to the earth by the gods

and requires the help of the gods to reascend.

Iamblichus' insistence on the paramount importance of the

gods and greater kinds in the life cycle of the human soul was fully

supported by his metaphysical interpretations of Plato's Phaedrus

and Timaeus. He reinterpreted the entourage of the Phaedrus and

the Demiurge's creation in the Timaeus so as to insure human reliance

on the gods. It was argued in section IIIA, above, that Iamblichus'

conception was the basis for that of Syrianus and Proclus. It can

now be seen that it was also a reaction to Plotinus' philosophy. As

such, Iamblichus' reinterpretation is a new and important turn in
neoplatonic religious philosophy. The need for divine intervention
and theurgy was tied to the metaphysics of Plato. From the time of
Iamblichus onward, philosphy and theurgy are inextricably linked.

Under this new interpretation, τόλμα is an inconsistent and
unnecessary doctrine. For Iamblichus the human soul is sent to earth
by the Demiurge himself in accordance with the necessary universal law
of the Timaeus, and every soul must descend.[84] But the Phaedrus shows
that each soul differs by its ability to control its passions and
glimpse true being. Thus, although every soul must descend, all souls
are not equal in the descent. A soul's inability to control its irrational nature is neither τόλμα nor the fault of the gods. For, according to Iamblichus, the Demiurge assured the equality of all souls
and their chances for eternal happiness by the sowing. It is up to
the souls to make their own way, but they do so through the help of
the gods and their intermediaries.[85]

Iamblichus' plan for the soul's descent includes a place for
the soul's vehicle. From the Timaeus, Iamblichus argued that the
vehicle was created by the Demiurge and placed by him into the circulation of the celestial gods. As the human soul was joined to the
divine soul, so the human vehicle was joined to the divine vehicle.[86]
From the Phaedrus, Iamblichus argued that vehicle of the human soul followed that of its leader-god. The difficulty that the human soul ex-
periences in attempting to follow its leader-god is caused not by the
soul's vehicle but by its irrational soul. The vehicle, being ethereal,
is like the god's vehicle. It follows that the human vehicle remains
akin to that of the god and can be used in the soul's reascent to him.

Notes to Section III

[1]Cf. Festugière (216-223).

[2]See Dillon (39 and 335-336). Cp. In Tim. Fr. 56 and Dillon (336-337).

[3]Both passages have been discussed in section I, above. Note that in both De An. I, p. 365, 15-16 and p. 372, 10-12, Iamblichus is hesitant about attributing this opinion to Plotinus; in the first passage, Iamblichus states that Plotinus does not completely (οὐ πάντῃ) agree that the soul is equivalent to intellect and in the second that "sometimes" (ἐνίοτε) Plotinus identifies the two. At De An. I, p. 377, 13-15, the hesitation is gone. The reason that Iamblichus can place Plotinus in a group of philosophers who do not distinguish between soul and intellect is probably not due to carelessness (since he has already stated that Plotinus does not definitely belong to this group) but to Iamblichus' tendency to oversimplify for the sake of the argument. On the correct view of Plotinus, who does distinguish between soul and intellect, see Smith (41-47).

[4]Festugière (258-260) translates In Tim. III, pp. 275, 26-278, 32.

[5]The distribution of souls around the stars will be discussed below in this section. See Proclus, In Tim. III, pp. 263, 22-265, 12.

[6]See especially De Myst. VIII 6, p. 269, 1-3 where Iamblichus claims that humans have two souls (rational and irrational) and that the rational soul is "from the first noetic." Cf. X 5, p. 290, 10-14. Both of these passages will be discussed in section IV below. For the bodiless human soul as ὑπερφυής, De Myst. I 10, p. 34, 10.

[7]The parentheses are Dillon's.

[8]Reading περὶ τὰς θείας δημιουργίας with the manuscripts FP. Usener suggested παρά for περί, and this reading is accepted by both Wachsmuth and Festugière. However, there is no need for the emendation. Plato had said that the Demiurge sowed the souls into the "organs of time" (Tim. 41e5), i.e., into the planets. Iamblichus is paraphrasing Plato. The phrase θείας δημιουργίας is a periphrasis for "the divine demiurges," i.e., the visible gods themselves (both above and below the moon) whom Plato calls νέοι θεοί (see In Tim. III, p. 310, 8-9).

[9]Cp. Proclus, In Tim. III, p. 276, 28-30: The soul "with its vehicle having been sown, becomes a citizen of the lunar or solar or some other circulation."

[10] Compare Proclus, In Tim. III, p. 275, 26-31 (partially

quoted above in this section).

[11] Proclus' playful use of the term φιλοθεάμονα here is reminiscent of In Tim. Fr. 54, where he says that Iamblichus μετεωροπολεῖ καὶ τάφανῆ μεριμνᾶ. See Dillon's note (335). Festugière, in his edition of Proclus' Timaeus commentary, also suspects that Proclus is referring to Iamblichus here (IV, p. 141 n. 2). The word φιλοθεάμων itself is Iamblichean. See Protrepticus p. 94, 13-14: "For only philosophers are φιλοθεάμονες of truth;" De Myst. V 21, p. 228, 13-14: "all the φιλοθεάμονας of theurgic truth;" and In Tim. Fr. 4: the missing fourth guest is "a φιλοθεάμονα of the noetic." Proclus is turning Iamblichus' own term back onto Iamblichus himself.

[12] Hence Proclus' comment at In Tim. III, p. 280, 23 that Plato refers not only to living creatures on the earth but also to those ἐν ἄλλοις στοιχείοις.

[13] Dillon (297 and 373-374). Cf. In Tim. Fr. 20.

[14] As Dodds (303-304) argues is the case for Proclus. Iamblichus certainly accepted astrology into his own system. See De Myst. IX 4. His very acceptance of cosmocrators (i.e., the planets in their capacity of ruling over human lives) is further proof. See De Myst. II 3, p. 71, 4 and Dillon (51), as well as In Tim. Fr. 11 and Dillon (275-276).

[15] Iamblichus suggests that each planet has a different influence in De Myst. I 18, p. 55, 6-7, where he states that the emanation (ἀπόρροια) from Saturn is συνεκτική but that from Mars is κινητική.

[16] See especially De An. I, p. 380, 6-29, discussed below in this section. See also Festugière (223 n. 2) and Dillon (255-256).

[17] In Festugière's edition of Proclus' Timaeus commentary, V, p. 155 n. 4.

[18] On the verb προβάλλειν see footnote #9 in section II, above.

[19] On the Greek word τελεστικόν, see Lewy (495-496), who gives three aspects of its definition: the word refers to (1) the purification of the soul, (2) the consecration of cult statues, and (3) the bringing of these statues to life. Each of these aspects is performed by a priest. In the present case, the first definition is meant. For Proclus (In Tim. III, p. 300, 13-20), the telestic life is superior to the philosophic life because the former "causes to disappear all stains from generation--as the Chaldaean oracles teach--and every opposing substance that the pneuma and irrational nature of the soul drag along." (Cf. Psellus, Exposition 1129c-1132c, where "the telestic science is the one purifying the soul from the power of matter.") The telestic life, therefore, is the life of

initiates who have succeeded in purifying their vehicle and have been united to the gods through theurgic ritual. (See section IV, below.) See also des Places, in his edition of the Chaldaean Oracles, pp. 168-169, and Festugière, in his edition of Proclus' Timaeus commentary, V, p. 177 n. 4.

[20]According to Dillon (287), Iamblichus considers Athena "the Soul of the Universe. She plays a demiurgic role, presiding over ἡ νέα δημιουργία. Apollo Iamblichus would posit as presiding over the Sun, rather than proceeding from it as Intellect, which for him is the role of Asclepius." See also Dillon (290-291).

[21]See, e.g., In Tim. Fr. 87, where Iamblichus states that προαίρεσις ἁμαρτάνει. It is interesting to note that in the passage from Proclus, the "living well or badly" exists along with the chosen life: "For each of the lives receives in addition the well and the badly" (p. 279, 23-24). This is in keeping with the myth of Er, in which the souls choose a life that is predetermined, i.e., the life they choose is good or bad when it is chosen. See expecially Rep. X.618b2-4.

[22]Iamblichus seems to believe in a similar connection between humans and gods (and indeed all the greater kinds) in De Myst. I 8, pp. 25, 16-26, 15. For Proclus, see In Tim. III, p. 276, 18-22.

[23]The translation is Dillon's (191).

[24]Compare In Tim. Fr. 76: the sublunary god, Ocean, "of whom the δραστήριοι φύσεις and the pneumatic elements, such as air and fire, partake." The "active natures" are probably the demons (cp. De An. I, p. 372, 18, where the acts of demons are called δραστήρια), although the word δραστήρια is used of other divine beings, such as angels and archangels, as Dillon (232) notes in another context. Thus, the god Ocean is seen as ruling over the boundaries of certain classes of the greater kinds. This doctrine reinforces the argument (given above in this section) that Iamblichus allotted Plato's "winged class that traverses the air" (Tim. 39e10-40a1) to the higher greater kinds, such as the archangels, angels, and heroes. (Cf. Proclus, In Tim. III, pp. 107, 30-108, 1.) Also, in In Tim. Fr. 76, Iamblichus declares the sublunary goddess, Tethys, to be participated by earth and water.

[25]At p. 263, 7, Proclus does mention a philosopher named Akylus. The name occurs only here. See Festugière's edition of Proclus' commentary, V, p. 137 n. 2.

[26]See below in this section.

[27]The passage is discussed in section II, above.

[28]That neoplatonists took τὸ πᾶν as referring to the souls and not to the Universe is clear from Proclus, In Tim. III, pp. 260,

26-261, 11 and especially p. 261, 4-5: "having organized all the multitude of these souls" (συστήσας οὖν τὸ πλῆθος πᾶν τῶν ψυχῶν τούτων).

[29]The subsequent passage in Proclus' commentary (pp. 261, 12-263, 22) is probably also Iamblichean. There Proclus argues that when Plato says that the Demiurge "divided the souls equal in number to the stars," Plato did not mean that there was only one soul for each star. This argument sounds like a standard neoplatonic one. For a neoplatonist, there are naturally more human souls than divine ones.

[30]The same point is made in In Tim. III, p. 307, 12-26. The "body" is, of course, the soul's vehicle, not the corporeal body.

[31]For the doctrine of ἀποκατάστασις or "restoration," see Dodds (301-303), where he cites Iamblichus' Protrepticus 16.5. Iamblichus certainly accepted the doctrine of ἀποκατάστασις both for the celestial bodies and for humans, but whether he made an argument similar to that made here by Proclus is impossible to know.

[32]Tim. 38e4-5: συναπεργάζεσθαι χρόνον.   Cp. In Tim. III, p. 72, 10-16.

[33]The Politicus myth is, for a neoplatonist, similar to the Timaeus' creation myth in several ways: (1) the regions of the cosmos were apportioned to different deities (Pol. 271d4-5 and 272e6-273a1); (2) demons acted as leaders of herds (ἀγέλαι) of living creatures (271d6-e2); (3) a fixed number of births were allotted to each soul (272e2-3); (4) a reference to God as "Demiurge and Father" (273b1-2); and (5) the eternity of the cosmos under the auspices of the Demiurge (273d4-e4).

[34]Dillon (374), in a different context, calls such combinations "'portamanteau' solutions."

[35]In his edition of Proclus' commentary, V, p. 94 n. 4.

[36]As noted by Festugière in his edition of Proclus' commentary, V, p. 112 n. 2.

[37]For ὁμοούσιος in Iamblichus' writings, see De Myst. III 21, p. 150, 7-9: "For if one thing comes about through two, it is totally ὁμοειδές, ὁμοφυές, and ὁμοούσιον." For ἰσάξιος, see p. 151, 5: ἰσάξιος γίγνεται τοῖς θεοῖς. Festugière, in his edition of Proclus' commentary, cites De An. I, p. 372, 23ff. See also Festugière (203 n. 3), where he states that Proclus' In Tim. III, pp. 245, 27-246, 10 "semble inspiré de Jamblique."

[38]For this text, see Festugière (246 n. 2).

[39]Iamblichus can justify his use of the feminine here by

pointing to Tim. 41e4-5: "having sown them (αὐτάς) into their
appropriate organs of time."

[40]That Proclus would follow Syrianus' commentary and not
check Iamblichus' himself is not unusual. Dillon (380) believes
that Proclus follows Syrianus at In Tim. III, pp. 277, 31-279, 2
(on the "first genesis"). See also Dillon (364-365). For the
"typical amplification by Syrianus of an Iamblichean formulation,"
see Dillon (257 and 262).

[41]See also Dillon (374).

[42]In his edition of Proclus' commentary, V, p. 101 nn. 1-3.
Festugière compares this passage to Iamblichus' theory given by
Proclus at pp. 234, 32-235, 9.

[43]Note that Proclus says: "But now (ἀλλὰ νῦν) Plato wishes
to refer the cause of the essence of souls to the Demiurge"
(In Tim. III, p. 233, 10-12).

[44]Thus, Iamblichus accepts some version of the σειρά, or series
of gods who rule over their greater kinds. See Dillon (291 and 416).

[45]The translation is Dillon's (195-197).

[46]As Festugière (216-217 n. 5) notes.

[47]Cf. Tim. 42a3-b2.

[48]However, it is by no means clear that there is such a
contradiction between these two Platonic works. "Necessity" in
the Timaeus has a peculiar sense. What is called "necessary"
should not be confused with what is logically necessary. Rather,
the word refers to those aspects of the universe over which the
Demiurge does not have complete control. See J. Burnet, Greek
Philosophy: Thales to Plato (1914; rpt. London 1932) 341-343;
F.M. Cornford, Plato's Cosmology (London 1937) 162-177; W.K.C. Guthrie,
A History of Greek Philosophy, V (Cambridge 1978) 272-274;
G.R. Morrow, "Necessity and Persuasion in Plato's Timaeus,"
Phil. Rev. 59 (1950) 147-163; rpt. in Studies in Plato's Metaphysics,
ed. R.E. Allen (New York 1965) 421-437; and A.E. Taylor, A Commentary
on Plato's Timaeus (Oxford 1928) 299-303, and Plato: The Man and
His Work, 6th ed. (1949; rpt. New York 1963) 454-456. Under this
interpretation of "necessary," it is possible that the natural law
of the Timaeus (that it is necessary for all souls to descend) is
compatible with the reason for the descent given in the Phaedrus
(that a failure in the soul causes the soul to fall). In other
words, given that the descent is required for the completion of
the universe, the best possible way for the Demiurge to bring about
this descent may make use of a failure in the soul itself.

[49]For Plotinus' changing attitude, see E.R. Dodds, Pagan
and Christian in an Age of Anxiety (Cambridge 1965), pp. 24-26.
See also Wallis (77-79).

⁵⁰This passage is discussed by Festugière (70); J.M. Rist,
Plotinus: The Road to Reality (Cambridge 1967), pp. 120-121;
and Smith (33 and 36 n. 24). Cf. A.H. Armstrong, "Plotinus,"
in The Cambridge History of Later Greek and Early Medieval Philosophy
(Cambridge 1967), p. 255.

⁵¹Discussed by Dodds (note 49, above) 26; Festugière (93-
94); Rist (note 50, above) 121-122; and Wallis (77-78).

⁵²As Dodds (note 49, above) 26 says. Cf. Wallis (78).

⁵³As Festugière (92) states: "Dans cette conception, le
péché originel est une sorte de péché de narcissisme: le prototype
céleste de l'âme s'eprend de sa propre image reflétée dans la
matière" (emphasis in the original). Cp. Wallis (78).

⁵⁴This passage is discussed by Dodds (note 49, above) 26;
Rist (note 50, above) 120; and Wallis (78-79).

⁵⁵On the "tension" in Plotinus' philosophy of the soul's
descent, see A. Tripolitis, The Doctrine of the Soul in the Thought
of Plotinus and Origen (Libra Press 1978) 54-58 and A.N.M. Rich,
"Body and Soul in the Philosophy of Plotinus," Journal of the History
of Philosophy 1 (1963) 2-3.

⁵⁶See especially Wallis (78-79).

⁵⁷For Porphyry's attempt, see Smith (35-39). Porphyry
seems to accept that the soul's first descent is necessary (not
voluntary) and that the soul is sent by god.

⁵⁸See Festugière (202 n. 2 and 211 n. 2).

⁵⁹See the notes to the translation of Festugière (209-210).

⁶⁰Later (De An. I, p. 378, 21-25), Iamblichus again uses
phraseology very similar to Plotinus' (IV.8.1.11-15). Cf., Festugière
(71), where the Greek texts are compared.

⁶¹Especially Plotinus' πρώτη ἑτερότης and Albinus'
αὐτεξούσιος διημαρτημένη κρίσις (375, 10-11). The case for the
Gnostics' παράνοια ἤ παρέκβασις is not as clear. As Festugière
(210 n. 2) points out, the words are not in Plotinus' treatise
"Against the Gnostics" (II.9). However, τόλμα is mentioned at
II.9.11.21. Cf. Armstrong (note 50, above) 244. There is ample
evidence that Plotinus and Iamblichus after him believed that the
Gnostics accepted τόλμα as the reason for the soul's descent.

⁶²For the view that "Iamblichus is simply recording two
different views of Taurus himself . . . and making somewhat
eccentric use of the common periphrasis 'those about X,'" see
J. Dillon, The Middle Platonists (Ithaca 1977), p. 245. As Dillon
also notes, the two views given as Taurus' are not contradictory.
Indeed, they are two mutually compatible ways of looking at the same

problem.

[63]Tim. 39e3-40a2; 41b7-c2; 92c5-9, all of which are cited
and translated by Festugière (73-74). Cf. Dillon (note 62,
above) 245, who cites the first passage. See also Plotinus IV.8.1.
40-50 and Festugière (74 n. 1).

[64]Festugière (77); Dillon (note 62, above) 246.

[65]Note that Iamblichus himself accepts such a class of
souls and distinguishes them from impure souls at De An. I, p. 379,
22-25 (αἱ καθαραὶ ψυχαὶ καὶ τέλειαι and αἱ ἐναντίαι) and p. 380,
23-29 (ἀπαθεῖς καὶ ἀκήρατοι and ἀπὸ τῶν ἐπιθυμιῶν ἄδην ἀναπεπλησμένοι
καὶ ἄλλων παθῶν μεστοί). The former passage was discussed in section
II, above; both passages will be discussed below in this section.

[66]See especially De An. I, pp. 454, 10-458, 21 (discussed
in section IV, below). For the "ancients" as "les fondateurs
(présumés) de la théurgie," see Festugière (263).

[67]The translation is Dillon's (89).

[68]Dillon (243-244) is certainly correct when he says that
the neoplatonic epithet θεῖος as applied to such philosophers as
Plato and (later) Iamblichus himself refers to these pure souls
who have passed the muster, as it were, in this life and gone on
to their rightful reward.

[69]Cf. IV.8.5.7-8: ὅλως τὸ ἑκούσιον τῆς καθόδου καὶ τὸ
ἀκούσιον αὖ. The descent is simultaneously voluntary and involuntary.

[70]See Festugière (76): "puisque . . . le monde est regardé
comme bon, il est légitime de croire que les âmes descendent
ἑκούσιοι."

[71]See Plato Phdr. 248c2: θεσμός τε ἀδραστείας ὅδε.

[72]Iamblichus believes that pure souls are neither judged
nor punished (De An. I, p. 456, 12-28). See section IV, below.

[73]See also Phdr. 248a1-b5, where Plato divides the human
souls into three groups: the first controls its horses and views
true being, the second is not as successful at handling its horses
but does glimpse true being somewhat, and the third is unable to
control its horses and fails to see true being.

[74]As Dillon (256) suggests, they can "earn a higher perch on
the celestial ladder."

[75]Compare the stages of initiation in Mithraism. See Lewy
(414-415 n. 51).

[76]The Forms exist in νοῦς, the third element of the noetic
triad. See In Phil. Fr. 4 and Dillon (37). Since νοῦς is also

the first element of the noeric realm, the Forms are said to be
produced in the noeric realm by the νοῦς: ὁ τρίτος (i.e., the
third element in the noetic triad) εἰδοποιίας ἐν νοεροῖς ᵗἐστιν
αἴτιος᾿ (In Phil. Fr. 4).

[77]See also Dillon (37-38).

[78]The translation is Dillon's (97).

[79]Dillon (253) notes that "the reference to 'some places'
in which Iamblichus has identified 'the great heaven' with the
Demiurge is probably to In Tim. Fr. 34." Proclus is misinterpreting
Iamblichus, however, as Dillon (38) points out. Iamblichus does
not identify the Demiurge with the whole noeric realm. He merely
says that the Demiurge embraces the whole noetic realm and uses it
in his creation of the cosmos. For the term ὑπεζωκώς, see
Dillon (252-253). As he notes, the Chaldaeans believed that this
entity was the Soul of the World. See Lewy (92 and n. 101).
As Lewy (92 n. 102) points out, Proclus considered the ὑπεζωκώς
"as the lowest god of the 'intellective (νοερά) hebdomad.'" Iamblichus
probably believed so as well: see Dillon (418-419). It is most
likely, therefore, that Iamblichus is not using the term ὑπεζωκυῖαν
in its technical sense in In Phdr. Fr. 5 (hence, his phrase οἷον
ὑπεζωκυῖαν) but simply to refer to a boundary between two realms.

[80]Iamblichus was alone in his opinion. See Dillon (389
and 400). The more common view was that the third hypothesis
concerned soul.

[81]Symp. 202d13-203a8. Cf. Dillon (400-401).

[82]Dillon (401) professes uncertainty about the nature of
the greater kinds' ascents and descents. He concludes that "since
such a descent did not involve contamination with matter, it
therefore involved no real separation from the intelligible
realm." Although Dillon does not say so, his view of the pure
descent of the greater kinds is in harmony with Iamblichus' claim
that pure human souls undergo a descent in which they are never
truly separated from the noetic realm (In Phaed. Fr. 5). However,
there is still a problem for Iamblichus. As was seen in section II,
above, certain demons do become contaminated by matter when they
descend. Moreover, in De Myst. II 7, pp. 83, 16-84, 3, Iamblichus
distinguishes three kinds of demon: good demons, punishing
(τιμωροί) demons, and evil (πονηροί) demons. Since this chapter of
the De Mysteriis concerns the supernatural manifestations (αὐτοψίαι,
p. 83, 10) of the greater kinds, it is evident that all three types
of demon descend. It seems likely that good demons (and probably
punishing demons as well) make a pure descent, as pure souls do.
Evil demons, like impure souls, do not. The evil demons have no
ruling allotment (ἡγεμονικὴν . . . λῆξιν, De Myst. IX 7, p. 282,
3-4) and wreak havoc upon human attempts to perform theurgic rites
(De Myst. III 31, pp. 176, 3-177, 6; cf. Lewy [273-275]). There
was a traditional belief in their existence, of course, and

Iamblichus must have felt compelled to include them in his metaphysical system. (The Chaldaeans believed in evil demons: see
Lewy [259-279; 235-238].) Evil demons, however, remain a
stumbling block to Iamblichus' assertion of the purity of the
greater kinds. Iamblichus would argue that it is the contamination
caused by matter that makes demons evil, but why should the elevated
soul of a greater kind be susceptible to such contamination?
Belief in the existence of evil demons probably became such an
embarrassment that Sallustius and Proclus denied their existence.
(See notes 28 and 29 in section II, above.)

[83]See Enn. IV.4.44 and Wallis (71-72).

[84]As Dillon (243) notes, the Iamblichean belief that every
soul must descend is in conflict with the Phaedrus myth. For
Plato, those souls who successfully follow god and see true being
are freed from pain (ἀπήμονα, Phdr. 248c4) for a thousand-year
cycle; they do not descend. Iamblichus and the neoplatonists
after him interpreted the Phaedrus differently. Iamblichus
probably based his interpretation upon that of the Chaldaean
Oracles. See section IV, below.

[85]Proclus follows Iamblichus' view both in the necessity
of the descent of the soul and in the rejection of τόλμα. See
Wallis (158).

[86]Cp. Proclus, In Tim. III p. 276, 19-22: "Whenever a
particular soul attaches itself to (συντάττη) a whole soul, its
vehicle also follows the vehicle of the divine soul, and, as the
soul imitates the intellection of the divine soul, so also its
body imitates the movement of the divine body."

IV. The Theurgic Role of the Vehicle in
Iamblichus' Religious Philosophy

In section I, it was argued that Iamblichus' conception of

the vehicle was directed against Porphyry's theories. Iamblichus

disagreed with Porphyry about the vehicle's composition, generation,

and ultimate fate. Whereas Porphyry held that the vehicle was made

up of mixtures from the celestial gods and, therefore, capable of

being dissolved back into those component parts, Iamblichus claimed

that the vehicle was made up from ether as a whole and was

indestructible. Porphyry argued that the vehicles of philosophers

were dispersed and that their rational souls existed on eternally as

separate entities. Iamblichus responded that all souls, even those

of philosophers and theurgists, must descend again into this realm.

In sections II and III, two preliminary studies were

undertaken. It was shown that Iamblichus devised a strict meta-

physical hierarchy in which the noetic gods and the Good beyond

them were accessible to humans only through the intervention of the

greater kinds and the visible gods. From the purified human souls

to the visible gods (and beyond), there is one continuity, one chain

of being connecting embodied human souls to their ultimate reward.

It was argued that this metaphysical system was based upon Plato's

Phaedrus myth. Each human soul was allotted a leader-god to which it

was connected by a series of greater kinds. The soul's salvation

depended upon these intermediary entities, and they could be reached

only through theurgy.

In this section, two questions which arose earlier in this

study will be answered: first, what becomes of the vehicle of the

soul when the rational soul separates from it, and, second, why does

Iamblichus hold his unique theory of the vehicle? These questions
will be answered by considering the role of the vehicle in the
religious philosophy of Iamblichus and by citing evidence from the
Chaldaean Oracles and from the works of Julian.

In Book X of his De Mysteriis, Iamblichus sets out to answer
Porphyry's question: "Could there be another unknown road to
happiness (εύδαιμονία)?" (X 1. p. 286, 1). From the context, it is
clear that Porphyry means a road other than theurgy.[1] Iamblichus
responds (p. 286, 2-3): "And what other reasonable ascent (εΰλογος
. . . ἄνοδος) to happiness could there be separate from the gods?"
For Iamblichus, happiness is assured only through theurgy, which unites
the theurgic practitioner to the gods (286, 3-11).

Iamblichus continues along the same lines in X 5. For
Iamblichus, liberation from fate occurs only through knowledge of
the gods (τῶν θεῶν γνῶσις, p. 290, 16-17). At 291, 10-12, this
γνῶσις is equated with union with the gods (θεία ἔνωσις) and is
called "the first road to happiness" (πρώτη τῆς εύδαιμονίας ὁδός).
Iamblichus continues (pp. 291, 12-292, 3):

> And this hieratic and theurgic gift of happiness is called
> the door to the demiurgic god or the place or courtyard
> of the Good. It causes first a purity of the soul far
> more perfect than the purity of the body, next a training
> of the rational faculty (διανοία) for participation in
> and vision of the Good and for a release of all things
> opposite, and after these things union with the gods, the
> givers of good things.

Thus, this γνῶσις or union, the greatest happiness for humans,
is caused by theurgy.[2] The theurgic rite--bringing with it the
purification of the soul, its liberation from fate, and its union
with the gods[3]--is the soul's road to salvation. Each of these
three phases occurs in the Chaldaean sacrament of elevation (ἀναγωγή),

a theurgic rite to which Iamblichus attached great importance.[4]

Thus, the theurgic rite with which Iamblichus is concerned in

De Myst. X 5 and which leads to εὐδαιμονία is the Chaldaean eleva-

tion.[5] An examination of this theurgic rite and of the Iamblichean

allusions to it will help to explain Iamblichus' theory concerning

the ultimate fate of the vehicle.

Lewy (177-226) has gathered and explained the various

fragments of the Chaldaean Oracles concerned with the elevation.

All of these oracles would have been known to Iamblichus, who is

said to have written a voluminous work interpreting the Chaldaean

Oracles.[6] The Chaldaean Oracles describe a theurgic ritual by which

the soul of a living human is separated from his body and is carried

aloft to the gods.[7]

The first phase of the elevation is the purification of the

soul.[8] What is purified is the soul's vehicle, which the Chaldaean

Oracles say is made up of portions of ether, the sun, the moon, and

the air.[9] The vehicle of the initiate has become contaminated by

matter during the initiate's sojourn on earth and is thus weighed

down and unable to ascend. Ritual purification will remove the

material pollution and allow the soul to rise.[10]

It is clear that although Iamblichus disagreed with the

Chaldaean interpretation of the vehicle's composition, he nonethe-

less agreed that purification performed a necessary prelude to

theurgy. In De Myst. III 31, Iamblichus sets out the teachings of

the "Chaldaean prophets."[11] According to them, the true gods[12]

associate with those purified through theurgy and eradicate every

evil and every passion in them (p. 176, 5-7). These gods shine

their light (ἐπιλάμπονται, p. 176, 7) upon the initiates and thereby
free them from passions and every disorderly motion (p. 176, 11-12).
However, initiates who are impure (ἀλιτήριοι, p. 176, 13-14) are
isolated from the gods and become associated with evil demons (pp.
176, 13-177, 6). Thus, purification is a necessary precondition for
theurgy; those who are not purified cannot take part in the
rites.

The illumination of the gods and its role in purification
are taken up again in De Myst. III 11.[13] Here Iamblichus is considering
the oracle of Apollo at Clarus, at which there is a fountain from
which the priestess drinks before she delivers the god's oracles.[14]
Iamblichus argues against the Stoics,[15] who think that a mantic
pneuma extends through the water (p. 124, 16-17). The true reason
for the water's mantic power, according to Iamblichus, is that the
god Apollo illuminates the spring (ἐπιλάμπον τὴν πηγήν, p. 125, 1-2)
and fills it with a mantic power. When the priestess drinks from
this spring, the water that has been illuminated produces a fitness
and purification of her luminous vehicle (ἐπιτηδειότητα μόνον καὶ
ἀποκάθαρσιν τοῦ ἐν ἡμῖν αὐγοειδοῦς πνεύματος, p. 125, 4-6) and
thereby renders her capable of receiving[16] the god. Thus, Iamblichus
upholds the importance of the purification of the vehicle as a
prelude to the actual contact with the god and the delivery of his
oracle. Of course, Iamblichus is here discussing not a Chaldaean
ritual but the operation of an oracle. Nevertheless, the order in
which the oracular rite unfolds and the importance of the illumination
of the god in the purification of the priestess's vehicle show that
even in such cases as this Chaldaean influence is present. For

Iamblichus, it seems, no contact with the gods is possible unless
the vehicle of the soul has been purified.[17]

The Chaldaean Oracles themselves combine the gods'
illumination and the vehicle's purification. Lewy (198-199)
summarizes the view of the Oracles in this way:

> The reception of the sun-ray effects the final purification
> of the soul. The divine fire does away with all the
> "stains" which had defiled her during her sojourn on
> earth. She recovers the state which was hers before her
> descent from her noetic place of origin.

For the Chaldaeans, this same ray lifts the soul upward to union
with the Sun god.

Again, similar concepts are found in the De Mysteriis. In
De Myst. I 12, Iamblichus argues against Porphyry's opinion that
the gods are subject to passions and are dragged down to earth by
theurgists. As in the passage on the oracle at Clarus, Iamblichus
states that the gods do not descend here but voluntarily illuminate
the theurgist (αὐτοθελής . . . ἔλλαμψις, p. 40, 17-18). By this
illumination, the gods call the theurgist's soul up to them, unite
his soul to them, and lead him around to the noetic principle; in
so doing, they separate his soul from his body (p. 41, 6-9). As
Lewy (188) notes, Iamblichus is speaking of the Chaldaean elevation.[18]

Thus, once the initiate's vehicle has been purified by the
illumination of the god, it can begin its elevation to that god.
Returning to De Myst. III 11 (the Clarus passage), one can see
clearly that these are two separate moments in the ritual. For,
the priestess is first purified by drinking the water that has been
illuminated and then she is illuminated by Apollo and united to
him (p. 125, 8-10).[19]

The Chaldaean Oracles specify the rays of the sun as the source of the uplifting power allotted to souls.[20] The rays of the sun surround the soul's vehicle and lift it toward and unite it with the god. For the Chaldaeans, the sun was the ruler of the ethereal realm and the center and connective of the planets.[21] Iamblichus, on the other hand, grants this power to elevate souls not merely to the sun but to all the visible gods and greater kinds. The reason for this difference can be traced to Iamblichus' desire to combine the teachings of the Chaldaean Oracles with those of Plato.

In De Myst. II 6, Iamblichus states that the gods and greater kinds differ in the gifts each allots to the soul of the initiate. The gods grant "health of body, virtue of soul, purity of intellect, and, in sum, an elevation (ἀναγωγήν) to our proper principles" (p. 81, 12–14). Again the gods are said to illuminate the soul with light (τὸ φῶς ἐλλάμπει, line 18). The gifts of archangels are inferior to these and their illumination is weaker (p. 82, 2–5). Those of angels are even more inferior (p. 82, 5–8), and so on. The higher the divinity to which the soul is attached, the greater the rewards of theurgy.[22]

In De An. I, pp. 454, 23–455, 5, Iamblichus considers which entities bring about the purification of the soul.[23] The ancients (i.e., the theurgists), he says, teach that purification is brought about "by the visible gods, most of all by the sun, and by the invisible demiurgic causes, and by all the greater kinds" (p. 455, 1–4). Here Iamblichus admits that of the visible gods the sun is the most responsible for the soul's purification and, therefore, for its ascent.[24] This notion is clearly influenced by Chaldaean

beliefs.

There are two questions to be answered here. First, why

does Iamblichus claim that all the visible gods and greater kinds

elevate the soul when the Chaldaean Oracles limit this uplifting

power to the sun itself? Second, how does Iamblichus combine his

doctrine with that of the Chaldaeans?

As was suggested above, the answer to the first question

is to be found in Iamblichus' interpretation of Plato's philosophy.

In De An. I, pp. 457, 22-458, 2, Iamblichus says:[25]

> According to the Timaeus of Plato, just as souls are sown
> differently by the Demiurge--some into the sun, others
> into the earth--in the same way they are led up
> the road up (ἄνοδον), each soul not going beyond its
> boundary with respect to the demiurgic sowing.

In section III A, above, it was argued that the demiurgic sowing

consisted of the placement of the soul and its vehicle into the

circulation of its leader-god. It was in this circulation that,

according to Iamblichus' interpretation of Plato's Phaedrus,

the human soul followed its god and viewed the Forms. And, it

was from this circulation that the soul descended into generation.

In the passage from the De Anima, it is clear that Iamblichus

believes that the human soul's reascent from generation follows

the reverse course. It ascends to its leader-god. Thus, if a

soul is mercurial, it will ascend to the god Hermes; if Apollonian,

to the sun; and so forth.[26] Moreover, since each god has a series

of greater kinds attached to it, the human soul can be united to

any of the greater kinds in the series. Thus, the human soul of a

theurgist can ascend proportionately according to the divine being

to which it attaches itself. Once reunited with its leader-god,
the human soul can once again follow in the god's entourage.

Along with this reascent to its leader-god, the human soul
undergoes a liberation from fate, the second phase of elevation
mentioned by Iamblichus. This phase is illustrated by a passage
from Plato's Timaeus and by Proclus' commentary on this passage.
In Tim. 41e1-3, Plato says: "having set [the souls] as on a
vehicle, the Demiurge showed them the nature of the universe and
told them the laws of fate." For a neoplatonist, Plato has described
two separate acts: first the attachment of the vehicle to the
rational soul, second the placement of soul and vehicle into the
realm of fate. Proclus, in a passage that was shown to be Iamblichean
in section III A, above, gives this interpretation (In Tim. III, p.
276, 5-8):

> Therefore, in order that souls with their vehicles may
> come under the realm of fate, it is necessary for them to
> descend and become associated with generation, which
> [descent] is second after the sowing.

Thus, the soul does not become subject to fate until after its
descent into this realm. First the soul is attached to its vehicle,
then the soul and its vehicle are "sown" into the celestial gods,
and finally (after these first two occurrences) the soul descends
and becomes subject to fate. In another passage, also based upon
Iamblichus' lost commentary[27] (In Tim. III, p. 266, 11-16),
Proclus says:

> For first they [i.e., the human souls] come into existence,
> then they are distributed around the divine rule, and
> third they are mounted on vehicles, view nature, and hear
> the fated laws. From which it is easy to see that for
> Plato souls are superior to fate in accordance with their
> highest life.

In the soul's reascent to its leader-god, the soul is
released from the laws of fate. Since, as Proclus says, souls
are above fate κατὰ τὴν ἀκροτάτην ἑαυτῶν ζωήν   (p. 266, 16),
it is only when souls are reattached to their leader-god and when
their vehicles follow along with the god's vehicle that the human
souls, released completely from generation, "escape the implacable
wing of fate" (p. 266, 19 = Ch. Or. Fr. 130). Thus, for Iamblichus,
the soul is still united to its vehicle when the theurgic rites
release it from fate.[28]

The "highest life" of the soul is, of course, its separated
life. And it is the purpose of the theurgic rite to free the soul
from its irrational nature so that it can live this separated life
(ἡ ψυχὴ ἄλλην ζωὴν ἀλλάττεται, De Myst. I 12, p. 41, 12), as will
be seen shortly.

But first, now that it has been established that Iamblichus'
attribution of the soul's ascent to all the celestial gods is due
to his interpretation of Plato's writings, it must next be shown how
Iamblichus reconciled the views of Plato with those of the Chaldaean
Oracles. Evidence for Iamblichus' reconciliation is found in two
orations of Julian (Oration IV, Hymn to King Helios and Oration V,
Hymn to the Mother of the Gods) and in Macrobius' Saturnalia I.17-23.[29]

Julian's two orations display a metaphysical system similar
to that of the Chaldaean Oracles.[30] The Chaldaean system included
three realms: the Empyrean, the Ethereal, and the Hylic. Each of
these realms has its own ruler: Aion, the Sun, and the Moon,
respectively. Each of these entities plays a role in the theurgical
elevation. The sun, of course, is responsible for the soul's ascent.

Aion is the source of the sun's light; the moon presides over the
realm of generation, to which the soul passes in its descent and
from which it returns in its elevation to the sun. The Chaldaeans
viewed Aion as an invisible sun existing in the highest (Empyrean)
realm. Aion was the Chaldaean's second god, ranked immediately
after the Father (the supreme deity). Thus, Aion sends to the sun
the noetic light of the Father, the Father himself being even
further removed from mortals. The light of the sun by which souls
are elevated is, therefore, empyrean. The link between the human
soul and the Father is guaranteed by the intermediaries of the three
rulers. Thus, in the Chaldaean elevation, the soul is united not
merely to the visible sun but also to the invisible sun, Aion, and,
thereby, to the Father. The three rulers play a part: the Aion
sends the light from the Father, the sun transmits that noetic light
to the ethereal realm, and the moon, as ruler of the hylic realm, aids
in the transmitting of this light to the earth.

Julian, in his Hymn to King Helios, discusses a similar,
though not identical, metaphysical system. The discrepancies between
the two systems will help to show the changes that Iamblichus made
in his reconciliation of the Platonic and Chaldaean systems.
Iamblichus transformed the three Chaldaean realms into three neoplatonic realms: noetic, noeric, and visible. For Julian divides
the universe into these three realms at IV.132CD.[31] In each of these
realms there is a "sun:" in the visible realm, the visible sun; in
the noeric, Helios; and in the noetic, the One (IV.132C-133C). The
One, described by a long, typically Iamblichean set of synonyms
(132D), is said to be the source of beauty, essence, perfection,

and union for the noetic gods (133B). Helios, in his turn, is
the source of the same goods for the noeric gods (133C), and the
visible sun for the visible gods (133CD). The One is, in short,
the ruler of the noetic realm, just as Helios is of the noeric
and the visible sun of the visible realm.

In the Chaldaean system, this first "sun" is Aion.[32]
Julian, therefore, equates Aion with the neoplatonic One. There is
a Iamblichean basis for this identification. In In Tim. Fr. 61,
Iamblichus interprets Plato's phrase "eternity remains in the One"
(μένοντος αἰῶνος ἐν ἑνί, Tim. 37d6) as meaning that Aion resides in
the Good (τἀγαθῷ). In other words, Aion (or eternity), of which
time is a moving image (εἰκώ . . . κινητόν τινα αἰῶνος, Tim. 37d5),
is a horizontal extension of the One; i.e., it exists on the same
level as the One.[33] This One, as Dillon (343) points out, is τὸ
ἀεὶ ὄν, the One mediating between the noetic realm below and the
realm of the One above.[34] Thus, Iamblichus has merged the Chaldaean
conception of the noetic god, Aion, with the Platonic conception
of eternity in such a way as to guarantee this god's mediatory
position between the ineffable One and the noetic realm (and, of
course, in such a way as to mirror Aion's role in the Chaldaean
system as an intermediary between the Father and the lower realms).
Aion, as the first member of the noetic triad, is the ruler of the
noetic realm.

Helios is, of course, Julian's main concern in his hymn.
In the Chaldaean system, the second ruler was the visible sun.
Iamblichus obviously interpreted the oracles differently. The
visible sun, in Iamblichus' conception, becomes the third ruler.

This interpretation may seem strained, but Iamblichus had his own Platonic reasons for this interpretation.[35]

Where does Helios, the second ruler, fit into Iamblichus' metaphysical scheme? Julian concentrates on four main attributes of this god, attributes that help to clarify Helios' position. First, Helios is said to proceed from the One (Or. IV.132D, 141D-142A, 144D, 156CD). That is to say, Helios is a vertical emanation of Aion. That this is a vertical and not a horizontal emanation is clear from the second of Helios' attributed, viz., that he is a noeric god and rules over the other noeric gods (Or. IV.133B, 133C, 138C, 156D). Helios is thereby placed in the realm beneath the noetic realm (the noetic realm being that over which Aion is said to rule). Third, Helios is called the mean or middle (μέσος) of the middle noeric gods (Or. IV.132D, 138C, 142A, 156D). By this, Julian means that Helios is the mean between the noetic and the visible gods (138D, 148AB). Julian explains the term μεσότης (138D) as "that which unites and leads together things that are separate" (τὴν ἑνωτικὴν καὶ συνάγουσαν τὰ διεστῶτα). Thus, Helios' role as the middlemost entity of the middlemost realm is to link the gods of the noetic realm with the visible gods. He is, there-fore, to be placed at the summit of the noeric realm just as Aion was placed at the summit of the noetic. From this position, Helios is not only the third member of the noetic triad (and therefore has immediate access to the noetic gods) but also is the first member of the noeric realm, over which he rules.[36]

This third attribute leads directly to Julian's fourth: Helios is demiurgic (Or. IV.132D, 141C). It is clear from Helios' position as the third moment of the noetic triad that Iamblichus

considered him to be the Demiurge. For, the third member of the

noetic triad is νοῦς, and it is νοῦς that, as Demiurge, "gathers

into one and holds within himself" the whole noetic realm.[37]

Although Julian does not explicitly state that Helios is the

Demiurge, his equating of Helios with Zeus makes this conclusion

inescapable. At IV.143D, Julian says that the demiurgic power of

Zeus (ἡ τοῦ Διὸς δημιουργικὴ δύναμις) coincides with Helios.

Furthermore, at both IV.136A and 149B, Julian explicitly equates

Zeus and Helios. It is clear from Macrobius Sat. I.23 that Iamblichus

also equated Helios and Zeus.[38] At Sat. I.23.5, after a quotation

from Plato's Phaedrus 246e4-247a2 (which describes Zeus as the

leader-god that all the other gods follow), it is said that Plato

wished this Zeus to be identified with Helios. It was shown in

section III B, above that Iamblichus thought that Zeus in this

passage was the Demiurge of the Timaeus (In Phaedrum Fr. 3). Thus,

for Iamblichus, Helios was the Demiurge.

As the Demiurge, Helios is the creator of all the visible

gods (Or. IV.141C, 146BC, 156D-157A). Thus, he is creator, too,

of the visible sun, the ruler of the visible realm. Indeed, the

visible sun has a special connection to Helios. For, it is

through the sun that Helios sends his own noetic rays into the

visible world (Or. 134AB):[39]

> Light itself is incorporeal. The solar rays (ἀκτῖνες)
> are the acme and flower of light. It is the opinion
> of the Phoenicians, who are wise and knowing in divine
> matters, that the sunlight which proceeds everywhere is
> the pure energy of pure νοῦς itself . . . and the pure
> energy of νοῦς shines forth into its own domain. (It
> is allotted the middle of the entire heaven.) Whence

> shining, it fills the heavenly spheres with all its
> vigor (εὐτονία) and illuminates everything with divine
> and pure light.

The light of the sun is filled with the energy of νοῦς, i.e.,

with that of Helios. Thus, the sun's rays are not merely ethereal

but the summit of ether (τοῦ πέπτου σώματος . . . τὸ κεφάλαιόν

ἐστιν ἀκτὶς ἀελίου, 132C). This is because the sun's rays are

endowed with those of Helios (140A, 151B, 156D). Moreover,

the νοῦ ἐνέργεια ἄχραντος, is allotted a position in the middle

of the visible realm. Thus, since the visible sun is allotted just

that position (135AB), it follows that the sun is a manifestation

of Helios in the visible realm. Just as Helios can be called the

offspring of the Good (i.e., of Aion, IV.144D), so the visible sun

is the offspring of Helios. He is Helios' active principle in this

realm.[40]

As such, the sun is the leader of the visible gods. He

is said to perfect and harmonize the powers that the other gods

give to the earth (Or. IV.138BC). He is situated in the middle

of the other planets "in order to assign goods to the other visible

gods who proceeded from him and with him" and to rule the planets,

stars, and the realm of generation (146C).[41] Thus, the other

visible gods are horizontal emanations of the sun, created by

Helios from the sun.[42]

The symmetry of Iamblichus' scheme, completely in harmony

with that discussed in section II, above, can now be seen. In

each realm (noetic, noeric, and visible) there is one ruler. Each

of these rulers is the primary god among others: Aion among the

noetic gods, Helios among the noeric gods, and the visible sun among the visible gods. Furthermore, each ruler is the vertical

emanation of the ruler before it: Helios from Aion, the sun from

Helios. Each ruler acts as a mean between two realms: Aion between

the ineffable One and the Noetic realm, Helios between the noetic

and noeric realms, the sun between the noeric and visible realms.

Helios is, thus, the middle of the middle, connecting all the

realms below him with those above him. Finally, each ruler is in

charge of gods at its own level, gods that are horizontal emana-

tions from itself: Aion over the noetic gods, Helios over the

noeric, the sun over the visible.[43]

The sun's power does not end with the visible gods. Helios,

through the sun, not only illuminates the entire encosmic and sub-

lunar realms but also brings into existence the angels of the sun

(Or. IV.142A and 141B). As Lewy (183 n. 27) points out, these

angels guide the solar rays and, thus, the ascending and descending

human souls. Helios creates not only angels but also all the

greater kinds (145C). Together with the moon, he is ruler over

the realm of generation (154D, 157A).

This, then, is Iamblichus' reconciliation of the doctrines

of Plato and of the Chaldaean Oracles. Human souls belong to one

celestial god, but each of the celestial gods are ruled by the

sun, around whom they revolve (146CD). Moreover, since each of

the celestial gods is a horizontal emanation of the sun,[44] the

powers of each god to elevate the human souls belonging to it are

derived from the rays of the sun and, therefore, from Helios.

Indeed, Helios perfects the gifts that these visible gods provide

(151B, 157A). Thus, although all the visible gods can elevate

souls, their power to do so comes through the sun from Helios.
In this way, the power can be said to belong particularly to the
sun but to be shared by all the visible gods.

The sun and the visible gods, then, can elevate the human
soul from the realm of generation and unite the soul to themselves.
This union is the theurgic ritual's third and final phase (after the
soul's purification and liberation from fate). It has already been
seen that the three rulers in the Chaldaean system play an important
role in the soul's elevation. The same is true of the three rulers
in Iamblichus' hierarchy. Julian says that Helios frees souls from
their bodies and leads them to the noetic realm (Or. IV.136B).
Helios purifies the soul by his light and leads them to their goal
(151CD). It now remains to show the method by which the human soul
is elevated and united to the gods.

The evidence of Julian's fifth oration can be used to
supplement that of his fourth. Here Julian introduces two further
deities--Cybele and Attis--and places them into the Iamblichean
hierarchy of the fourth oration. Cybele, the mother of the gods,
is the source of the noeric gods; she is the mother and wife of
Zeus (i.e., of Helios) (Or. V.166AB, 179D-180A). She is therefore,
a noetic goddess, originally prior to Helios but emanating to his
level. At his level (Διὸς σύνθωκος, Or. V.166B, cf. 170D, 179D),
since she holds the causes of the noetic gods, Cybele is the source
of the noeric gods; that is, she transfers the noetic cause to the
noeric gods. As Wright (I, p. 463 n. 3) points out, she is the
noetic equivalent of the noeric Athene: Cybele is providence
(πρόνοια) for the noetic gods.[45] Thus, since Athene is an emanation

from Helios (Or. IV.149CD), Cybele is an emanation from Aion, the

ruler of the noetic gods. She is his active principle and descends

into Helios' realm.

Attis, on the other hand, is a noeric god (Or. V.165D).

As such, he is under the rule of Helios. And indeed, Julian sets

out to describe the relationship existing between these two deities.

Helios[46] is "the father and master" of the immaterial cause of the

enhylic forms (165A), just as Attis is the god who joins together

the sublunar enhylic forms and unites them to the cause set above

matter. The distinction being drawn here is one between the Forms

themselves and the Forms-in-matter existing below the moon. Iamblichus

(In Phil. Fr. 4) places Forms in the third moment of the noetic realm,

i.e., in νοῦς (and at the disposal of the Demiurge). According to

In Parm. Fr. 2, Iamblichus considered the enhylic forms to be the

subject of Plato's sixth hypothesis (after irrational souls in the

fifth and just before matter in the seventh). It is clear, then,

that Julian's distinction is based firmly upon Iamblichean principles.

Helios, the Demiurge, controls the Forms (which exist at his level)

and Attis the enhylic forms (which exist in the encosmic realm).

Attis is, therefore, the creative activity of Helios capable

of descending into the encosmic realm (a descent that Helios, as

transcendent Demiurge, cannot make). As Julian says, Attis is

"the essence of the creative and demiurgic νοῦς, which [essence]

creates everything as far as lowest matter" (Or. V.161C). Attis,

then, is like Cybele in that both are emanations from their realm's

ruler and proceed into the next lower realm.

Julian associates both Cybele and Attis, along with Helios,

with the soul's descent to and ascent from generation. At the
Hilaria, a feast dedicated to Attis and held at the time of the
vernal equinox, human souls can hasten toward the life-producing
goddess (ζωογόνον . . . θεόν, Or. V.169BC), that is, to Cybele
(cf. 168A). At this time, Attis halts his own descent[47] and human
souls "are elevated to the gods themselves" (ἐπὶ δὲ τοὺς θεοὺς
αὐτοὺς ἀναχθείσης, 169D).

How can human souls follow Attis? Attis is said to be
similar to Helios' rays (ταῖς ἡλιακαῖς ἀκτῖσιν ἐμφερεῖ, 165C).[47]
Attis represents Helios' demiurgic power immanent in the encosmic
realm. Thus, since Helios' light (given to the realm of generation
through the visible sun) is the "pure energy of pure νοῦς itself"
(Or. IV.134AB) and since Attis is "the essence (οὐσία) of the creative
and demiurgic νοῦς" (Or. V.161C), it follows that Attis and Helios'
rays are similar in that each informs a particular demiurgic and
noeric quality of Helios immanent in this realm. Furthermore,
the sun's rays are the summit of ether (Or. IV.132C). Thus, the
solar rays partake of two realms: visible and noeric. Attis, who
follows Helios' rays down to the realm of matter, is the active
noeric element.

Helios' uplifting (ἀναγωγοί) rays are related to (ἔχειν
οἰκείως) human souls who desire to be freed from the realm of
generation (Or. V.172AB, 172C). Helios elevates (ἀνάξει) them "by
the invisible, completely incorporeal, divine, and pure essence
situated in his rays" (διὰ τῆς ἀφανοῦς καὶ ἀσωμάτου πάντη καὶ
θείας καὶ καθαρᾶς ἐν ταῖς ἀκτῖσιν ἱδρυμένης οὐσίας, Or. V.172B).
This essence is, as has been seen, Attis. Helios' light is, then,

a conduit through which Attis can descend and lift pure souls
upward to Helios. At Or. V.172D-173A, Julian makes the relationship
between Helios and Attis clear. Speaking from Chaldaean doctrine,
he says that Helios elevates (ἀνάγων) human souls through the
intermediary of Attis.[49] Nevertheless, it is not only through Attis
that souls are elevated. Helios' rays themselves also have this
uplifting power (172C). This power comes from Helios' "visible
and invisible energies," that is, through the visible powers of
the visible sun and from the invisible powers prior to the sun,
powers that are both noeric and noetic.

There is, therefore, a complete chain of gods from the One
to this realm, a chain that includes active intermediaries capable
of assisting purified souls in their ascent.[50] These souls are, in
accordance with the Iamblichean doctrine, purified by the light of
Helios (Or. IV.151C).[51] This purification, as has been shown,
involves the soul's vehicle, which, like the sun's rays, is ethereal.
The ethereal rays of the sun (originating from Helios) and the
active essence in those rays (i.e., Attis) aid in the ascent of the
human soul, which is itself attached to its ethereal vehicle. Thus
the rays of Helios are "related to" (οἰκεῖαι) the purified soul on
two levels. First, both the rays and the soul's vehicle are ethereal.
Second, Attis as pure νοῦς and that part of the sun's light that
derives from Helios (who is νοῦς) are similar to the rational soul,
which has a noeric component.[52]

Julian gives the following account of the soul's elevation
(Or. IV.152AB):

The more divine gifts [of Helios] --as many as he gives

> to souls, freeing them from the body, then elevating
> (ἐπανάγων) them to the kindred substances (συγγενεῖς
> οὐσίας) of the god, and providing the subtlety and vigor
> of his divine rays as a sort of vehicle for the soul's
> safe descent into generation-- [these gifts] let others
> hymn worthily but let them be believed rather than proven
> by us.

There are three points to be noted here. First, the doctrine

here is a religious dogma to be accepted on faith. The dogma is,

of course, Chaldaean, as the word ἐπανάγων proves.[53] Second,

Helios' rays are like (οἷον) the soul's vehicle and provide a

conduit for the Soul's descent and, therefore, for its subsequent

reascent.[54] The ethereal ray and the ethereal vehicle unite, and

the uplifting powers from Helios and Attis cause the soul--now

freed from the corporeal body--to ascend. Third, the kindred

substances to which the rays lead the soul are the ethereal bodies

of the visible gods.[55] This, too, is in accordance with the

Iamblichean doctrine of the soul's return to its leader-god. From

there the soul ascends to the noetic.[56]

The two orations of Julian show how Iamblichus conceived

of the human soul's union with its leader-god, a union brought about

by the theurgic ritual. The soul ascends, with the help of the

greater kinds and Attis, to its god via Helios' rays. In this

conception, the ethereal vehicle is the receptor of the divine

light. The light is the conduit for the vehicle and is the source

of the uplifting noeric energy. The light purifies the vehicle and

makes the rational soul fit for union with the gods. In this way,

Iamblichus combined metaphysics and theurgy and changed the direction

of neoplatonic philosophy.

It is now time to return to the first of the two questions

raised at the beginning of this section: what happens to the

vehicle in the soul's ascent? Certain passages from Iamblichus'

De Mysteriis and Platonic commentaries provide the evidence necessary

for answering this question.

It was shown in section I, above, that the fate of the

immortal vehicle is tied up with that of the irrational soul, which

is also immortal (In Tim. Fr. 81). There it was also argued that the

rational soul is capable of an existence separated from both the

vehicle and the irrational soul. The rational soul can ascend higher,

while the vehicle and irrational soul remained preserved in the

encosmic realm (De An. I, p. 384, 26-27). Finally, it was shown that

the separated rational soul contained a rational faculty (διάνοια)

and a noeric faculty (κατὰ νοῦν διάθεσιν, De An. I, p. 457, 13-14).

The vehicle and irrational soul are the organs for the soul's

lower functions. The vehicle controls the functions of sense-

perception and imagination;[57] the irrational soul such functions as

appetite, desire, etc.[58] These lower, irrational faculties are

useless in the upper realms and, indeed, could be detrimental to

its pure existence there. Thus, the soul that wishes to ascend

must divest itself of these faculties.

It has already been shown that the vehicle, which houses

both the rational and irrational souls, is purified and elevated

by the divine light. The vehicle also has a second function in

the soul's elevation. In the theurgic act, Iamblichus says

(De Myst. III 14, p. 132, 11-17), the gods illuminate

> the ethereal and luminous vehicle that surrounds the
> soul. From this [illumination] divine images take hold
> of the imaginative power (φανταστικὴν δύναμιν) in us,

images moved by the will of the gods. For the whole life
of the soul and all the powers in it are moved subject
to the gods, as the soul's leaders will.

When the vehicle is illuminated by the light from the soul's

leader-god, all external and internal stimuli to the vehicle

cease; only images from the god are impressed upon it. The

suppression of the lower faculties is complete. In De Myst.

III 6, pp. 113, 7-114, 2, Iamblichus claims that when a person is

illuminated by the gods, no sense-perception (αἴσθησις), no

consciousness (παρακολούθησις), no intuition (ἐπιβολή) takes place

in the vehicle. Indeed, such a person cannot partake of emotion,

ecstasy, or any errors from imagination. That is to say, all the

lower mental functions that do not belong essentially to the rational

soul are useless.[59]

The vehicle's second theurgic purpose, therefore, is to be

filled with divine images.[60] These images prevent any material

images or sense-impressions from occurring within the vehicle and

thus effectively block out any irrational activities. The rational

soul, freed from all irrational impulses, can now operate at its

proper noeric level.

At De Myst. III 14, p. 133, 3-4, Iamblichus states that

the higher faculties are indeed alert: "the soul's attentive

faculty (προσοχή) and discursive thought (διάνοια) are conscious

of what occurs."[61] Thus, for the soul's actual union with its

leader-god, only the psychic faculties necessary for such union

are active.

Iamblichus has more to say about the higher faculties

involved in the soul's union with the gods in two fragments from

Phaedrus and Timaeus commentaries. These fragments, taken together
with Iamblichus' blending of the Phaedrus and Timaeus myths, provide
the evidence necessary for showing how Iamblichus conceived the
immortality of the vehicle and irrational soul.

In In Phaedrum Fr. 6, Iamblichus interprets Plato's
description of the true beings in the supercelestial place (Phdr.
247c3-d1). Plato says that these Forms are seen only by the soul's
governor (ψυχῆς κυβερνήτῃ μόνῳ θεατῇ, 247c7), by which Plato
means the soul's νοῦς. [62] Iamblichus, however, takes the term
κυβερνήτῃ in a different sense. For Iamblichus, the governor differs
from the charioteer (ἡνίοχος, see, e.g., Phdr. 247e5). Iamblichus
calls the governor the soul's One (τὸ ἓν τῆς ψυχῆς) and the
charioteer the soul's νοῦς. Thus, it is not the soul's noeric
faculty that is the contemplator (θεατής) of the Forms, but the
soul's One, the governor. For Iamblichus, the governor is more
perfect (τελειότερος) than the charioteer and the horses (i.e.,
than the lower rational and the irrational faculties). "For the
soul's One is naturally united to the gods" (τὸ γὰρ ἓν τῆς ψυχῆς
ἐνοῦσθαι τοῖς θεοῖς πέφυκεν)."

In Phaedrum Fr. 6, therefore, presents a level of the soul
higher than its noeric capacity. This higher level is the psychic
equivalent of the One. As Dillon (253) puts it: "A special faculty
of the soul was required, to be the receptacle of mystical inspiration
from the gods, and to answer in the microcosm of the individual to
the realm of the One in the macrocosm." The soul's One was the
soul's means of being united with the higher noetic entities, even
with the One itself. Given Iamblichus' passion for detail in his

metaphysical system, it is by no means surprising that he would

postulate the need for a higher faculty in the human soul capable

of contemplation at the higher levels. It is equally to be

expected that he would find a way to foist the origin of the

doctrine of this higher faculty onto Plato himself. He found his

opportunity in Plato's casual use of κυβερνήτῃ in the Phaedrus.

The soul's One alone is the organ for the contemplation of the

Forms.

That the soul's One is not a separate faculty but an integral--

though higher--part of the rational soul is clear from In Tim. Fr. 87.

Here, after arguing against Plotinus that no part of the soul remains

above generation and impassible, Iamblichus draws upon Plato's

Phaedrus myth as further proof of his position. The soul's charioteer

(ἡνίοχος) is its highest part (κεφαλαιωδέστατον). It is the

governor (διακυβερνῶν) of an individual's entire being and contemplates

with its own head the "supercelestial place"[63] (τῇ ἑαυτοῦ κεφαλῇ

τὸν ὑπερουράνιον τόπον ὁρῶν). Thus, it seems that if Iamblichus

is being consistent between the two Platonic commentaries, Iamblichus

considers the soul's One as the charioteer's "head," i.e., as the

rational soul's highest part. As such it is equivalent to the

Chaldaean ἄνθος τοῦ νοῦ.[64]

Iamblichus' explanation of the role of the charioteer in

the soul's union with the gods depends upon his interpretation of

the Phaedrus. The charioteer, who "with his own head" views the

Forms in the noetic realm, is said to be made similar to the "great

leader" of the gods. The phrase μέγας ἡγεμών derives from Phdr.

246e4, where it refers to Zeus. It will be recalled that Iamblichus equates this deity with the Demiurge. It is he that all the other

gods (together with their entourage of greater kinds and human

souls) follow in order to contemplate the Forms. Thus, the charioteer,

by means of the soul's One, can be united to the Demiurge and view

the Forms. For Iamblichus concludes:[65]

> And if the charioteer is the highest element in us, and
> he, as is said in the Phaedrus, sometimes is carried aloft
> and raises "his head into the region outside" [Phdr.
> 248a2-3], while at other times he descends and (fills his
> pair) with lameness and moulting, it plainly follows that
> the highest element in us experiences different states
> at different times.

It follows that the soul's charioteer (i.e., the rational

soul) ascends and descends as an entirety. Its highest part (here

called its head) is the soul's One, and it glimpses the Forms in

"the region outside," i.e., in the noetic realm. It does so by

having its vehicle and irrational soul follow the Demiurge in the

entourage of the soul's leader-god. Note that Iamblichus says that

the rational soul alone--not the vehicle or the irrational soul--

enters the noetic realm. As Iamblichus says in In Phaedrum Fr. 6,

the soul's One is a contemplator of the Forms "not because it grasps

the noetic realm as if it were different from it but because it is

united to that realm." The soul's One is that part of the rational

soul that undergoes union with noetic entities.

In Iamblichus' interpretation of the Phaedrus myth, the

soul's vehicle (together with the irrational soul that is attached

to it) remains in the divine entourage while the rational soul

(conceived of here as the charioteer) can, as it were, poke its head

into the noetic realm. The vehicle and irrational soul, therefore,

remain below. They do not ascend to the noetic.

A passage from Proclus (In Tim. III p. 276, 19-22) helps
to explain the vehicle's situation:

> Whenever the partial [i.e., human] soul attaches itself
> to the whole [i.e., to the divine soul], its vehicle also
> follows the vehicle of the divine soul, and just as the
> soul imitates the intellection of the divine soul, so
> also its body imitates the movement of the divine body.

The vehicle's ultimate fate is to be reunited with the ethereal
vehicle of the visible god, the soul's leader-god. There the
vehicle and irrational soul remain, purified and free from all
irrational activity, while the rational soul mounts even higher.

As the vehicle waits below, the rational soul by means of
its highest part is united to the Demiurge.[66] But, as the term
τὸ ἕν τῆς ψυχῆς suggests, the rational soul is capable of even
a higher existence, as three passages from the De Mysteriis show.

In De Myst. V 20, p. 228, 2-12, Iamblichus states that it
is possible, although most rare, for a theurgist to be united with
hypercosmic gods. Such a union, however, occurs only to theurgists
who have perfected their art over a great amount of time. In De Myst.
V 22, pp. 230, 14-231, 2, the summit of the hieratic (i.e., theurgic)
art is the ascent to the One, but such an ascent occurs to an
exceedingly small number of priests and then only late in their lives.
Finally, in De Myst. X 7, p. 293, 1-4, Iamblichus claims that the
Egyptians believed the highest good for mortals is union with the One.

The rational soul of a theurgist can in some rare cases
separate itself from the vehicle and ascend to the One itself. On
the basis of Julian's orations, it would seem most likely that the
rational soul ascends to the One (or Aion) both through the rays
of Aion which are showered on the Demiurge (Helios) and through

Cybele, who like Attis descends from her own realm to assist
ascending souls. While the rational soul soars ever higher, its
vehicle remains under the protection of the leader-god's vehicle.
When the soul descends again, it re-enters its purified vehicle and
makes its pure descent back into the realm of generation
(In Phaedonem Fr. 5).

This, then, is the manner in which Iamblichus conceived the
immortal existence of the vehicle separated from the rational soul.
It is not that the vehicle exists "in the purity of the noetic realm"
or that it exists "eternally in the atmosphere as a daemon of some
grade."[67] The vehicle simply remains united to the vehicle of the
soul's leader-god.

It now remains to answer the second question raised at the
beginning of this inquiry: why did Iamblichus hold this unique view
of the vehicle's immortality. Again, the answer depends upon his
religious philosophy and upon his concern with the Chaldaean Oracles.

It was argued in section I, above, that Iamblichus' belief
in an immortal vehicle was opposed to Porphyry's doctrine that the
vehicle of the philosopher was dispersed back into the elements from
which it was constituted. Porphyry, according to Proclus, In Tim.
III, p. 234, 26-30, used as a basis for his doctrine the teachings
of the Chaldaean Oracles (Fr. 61e). Iamblichus, therefore, must
have combatted Porphyry's theories by referring to the Chaldaean
Oracles and showing the correct interpretation of them.[68]

Several passages from Iamblichus' De Anima help to shed
light on what was at issue. In De An. I, pp. 456, 12-457, 6,
Iamblichus discusses the judgment, punishment, and purification of

human souls at the time of their death. As Festugière (243 n. 1)

points out, this passage contrasts the views of the ancients (i.e.,

the theurgic priests) with those of the "Platonists and Pythagoreans"

(p. 456, 20-21), among whom Iamblichus includes Plotinus.[69] The

ancients, Iamblichus says, claim that some souls do not undergo

judgment, punishment, and purification, whereas the Platonists and

Pythagoreans claim that all souls do. The souls that the ancients--

and Iamblichus--would free from judgment, punishment, and purification

comprise the class of pure souls, which were discussed in section III

B, above. They are ἀπόλυτοι καὶ ἀμιγεῖς καὶ ἀδέσποτοι παντελῶς

καὶ αὐταὶ ἑαυτῶν οὖσαι καὶ πεπληρωμέναι τῶν θεῶν (p. 456, 17-18),

τὰς ἀχράντους ψυχὰς καὶ τὰς ὁμονοητικῶς συναφθείσας τοῖς θεοῖς

(p. 456, 23-24), and θεοῖς συνέπονται (p. 457, 2).[70] These

descriptions mark such souls as pure souls of the theurgists who for

a time were able to escape from the cycle of births and retain their

purity even in the realm of generation.

This doctrine, which makes a certain class of souls free

from the need of punishment for sins committed in an earlier corporeal

life is a Chaldaean one.[71] It is a doctrine that, as has been shown,

both Iamblichus and Porphyry accept. However, as was noted in

section I, above, there is another doctrine which Iamblichus accepts

and Porphyry rejects and which leads Iamblichus to adopt his theory

of the immortal vehicle. It can now be seen that Iamblichus found

corroboration for this doctrine in both Plato's Phaedrus and the

Chaldaean Oracles.

In De An. I, p. 457, 15-16, Iamblichus says that the ancients

"correctly give to it [i.e., the human soul] a superintendence

over things here, but Porphyry removes this [superintendence]
from it." The doctrine of the προστασία τῶν τῇδε is an important
one for Iamblichus. Human souls, once they became purified, did
not escape the cycle of births forever but returned to this lower
realm and returned for an honorable purpose. In De An. I, p.458,
17-21, Iamblichus compares the beliefs of the ancients with those
of the Platonists:

> According to the ancients, when souls have been freed from
> generation, they together with the gods govern (συνδιοικοῦσι)
> the universe, but according to the Platonists they contemplate
> the god's realm. Similarly, according to the former they
> together with the angels administer the universe, but
> according to the latter they revolve with them
> (συμπεριπολοῦσιν).

The distinction that Iamblichus is drawing is based (as the
words συνδιοικοῦσι and συμπεριπολοῦσιν show)[72] on Phdr. 245bc.
According to Plato, human souls sometimes "mount higher and govern
all the cosmos" (μετεωροπορεῖ τε καὶ πάντα τὸν κόσμον διοικεῖ,
246c1-2). For Iamblichus, these souls are the purified souls who
are able to view the Forms in the noetic realm.[73] Where the
Platonists go astray, according to Iamblichus, is in failing to
grasp the significance of the role of purified souls once they
return to the lower realm. These souls do not merely attain a passive
union with the gods, but having been purified by and united to the
gods, they return to this lower realm to help those less fortunate
souls still in it. As Iamblichus said of these purified souls at
De An. I, p. 380, 7-9: they descend "for the preservation, purification, and perfection" of this realm.

Thus for Iamblichus, both Plato's Phaedrus and the Chaldaean
Oracles provide the basis for the belief that all souls must descend

again.[74] Iamblichus' mention of angels at <u>De An</u>. I, p. 458, 20,

helps to clarify the position of such purified souls and to under-

score the Chaldaean influence on Iamblichus' doctrine.

Lewy (220 nn. 173 and 175) discusses two Chaldaean Oracles

(Frr. 137 and 138) that deal with the celestial rank accorded

to theurgists after their deaths. In the first oracle (from Proclus,

<u>In Rep</u>. II, p. 154, 17ff), theurgic priests (τελεστικοί) are allotted

the τάξις of angels: "'living as an angel in power,' (ἄγγελος ἐν

δυνάμει ζῶν) as the oracle says." In the second oracle (from

Olympiodorus, <u>In Phaed</u>. 10.14.8-10), it is said:

> But Plato does not wish the souls of the theurgists to
> remain forever in the noetic realm but to descend into
> generation, concerning which souls, the oracle says:
> "in the angelic space" (ἀγγελικῷ ἐνὶ χώρῳ).

Iamblichus has these two oracles in mind in <u>De Myst</u>. II 2,

p. 69, 8-17:

> Because of the good will of the gods and the illumination
> of their light, the soul often progresses even higher and
> is elevated (ἀναγομένη) to the greater, angelic order
> (τάξιν τὴν ἀγγελικήν). At that time, it no longer remains
> in the boundaries of soul, but is completely perfected
> into angelic soul and pure life . . . But if it is
> necessary to speak the truth, the soul is always defined
> according to one nature but, by associating itself with
> causes preceding it, the soul is united to some entities
> at one time and to others at others.

The purified soul can range from generation to the gods themselves

(pp. 68, 8-69, 6). As a reward for its pure life, it is granted

to the purified soul to dwell with the angels after its death

(i.e., at the end of its corporeal existence on earth). At such

time, the soul is above the normal τάξις of human souls. However,

since Iamblichus must insist on preserving the differences between different classes of soul (see section II, above), he carefully

points out that this union with the angels does not mean that the

human soul even of the theurgist is equal to an angelic soul. The

human soul belongs to its own τάξις (ὥρισται μὲν ἀεὶ καθ' ἕν τι,

p. 69, 16) but can be elevated higher by the gods.[75] Thus, for

Iamblichus, the soul of the theurgist exists with the angels and

together with them aids other human souls wishing to be elevated.

It has already been seen that the rational component of

purified human souls is capable of a separate existence in the

noetic realm and even in the realm of the One itself.[76] In the

encosmic realm, however, these souls--like the visible gods and

greater kinds--require a vehicle. For Iamblichus, this was the

soul's original vehicle, which, linked to its irrational soul and

already purified by the divine rays, remained attached to the

vehicle of the soul's leader-god. Thus, Iamblichus' conception of

the immortality of the vehicle is based upon his interpretation of

two Chaldaean doctrines: the doctrine of the soul's purification

and elevation to the gods and the doctrine of the purified soul's

return to and governance over the realm of generation.

Notes to Section IV

[1]As Scott (86-87) notes.

[2]Scott (91-92) fails to see this point, and this failure
leads him to alter Iamblichus' text at p. 290, 16-17. Scott
thinks that Iamblichus' statement that "release from the bonds
of fate" (290, 15-16) can occur only through θεῶν γνῶσις is
contradicted by what Iamblichus says at 291, 10-15, viz., that
this knowledge of the gods is the "first road" to happiness.
For Scott, "the hieratic and theurgic gift of happiness" (291,
12-13) represents a second, completely separate road to happiness.
He therefore takes the θεῶν γνῶσις, not as theurgy, but as
philosophical contemplation like that of Plotinus and Porphyry.
Such a view, however, runs counter to the accepted belief that
Iamblichus opposed Plotinus and Porphyry in this matter. See
De Myst. II 11, pp. 96, 13-97, 11, quoted in section III B,
above; Dillon (28-29); and Dodds (xx). Scott, however does not
believe that Iamblichus was the author of the De Mysteriis. Note
that Julian, Or. IV.180B, calls ἡ τῶν θεῶν γνῶσις the chief
happiness for human. beings.

[3]Cf. De Myst. I 12, pp. 41, 16-42, 1: κάθαρσιν παθῶν
καὶ ἀπαλλαγὴν γενέσεως ἑνωσίν τε πρὸς τὴν θείαν ἀρχὴν ἡ διὰ
τῶν κλήσεων ἄνοδος παρέχει τοῖς ἱερεῦσι; and X 7, p. 293, 7-8:
ψυχῆς κάθαρσις καὶ ἀπόλυσις καὶ σωτηρία are the concerns of
the theurgist.

[4]On the sacrament of ἀναγωγή, see Lewy (177-226). For
Iamblichus' interest in it, see Lewy (487-489). Iamblichus combined
the Chaldaean ἀναγωγή with Platonic and Hermetic doctrines. See
De Myst. I 1 and 2. Cf. Lewy (463-464). On the necessity of theurgy,
see De Myst. III 21.

[5]Note that the theurgic rite is called ἀναγωγή at De Myst.
X 6, p. 292, 17. This usage is cited by Lewy (487) as Chaldaean.

[6]Damascius, Dub. et Sol. I, p. 86, 5-6, refers to the 28th
book of Iamblichus' Chaldaean Theology. Damascius also refers to
this work at I, p. 154, 13-14. For allusions by other authors,
see Dillon (24). For the importance of the Chaldaean Oracles to
Iamblichean philosophy, see des Places' edition of the Chaldaean
Oracles, pp. 24-29.

[7]The sacred ritual consisted of at least three officiants:
the priest, the κλήτωρ (who invokes the gods), and the δοχεύς
or initiate whose soul was caused to ascend through the agency
of the gods summoned by the priest and κλήτωρ. See Lewy (39-40,
467-471).

[8]Lewy (178-184).

156

9
See Lewy (178 n. 4 and 182-183).

[10]See Lewy (183-184).

[11]Χαλδαίων . . . προφητῶν, p. 176, 2, i.e., Julian the
Chaldaean and Julian the Theurgist, the authors of the Chaldaean
Oracles. See Lewy (273 and n. 53) and des Places (144 n. 1).

[12]Iamblichus calls these gods "the givers of the only
goods" (τῶν ἀγαθῶν . . . μόνως δοτῆες, p. 176, 3-4). This
phraseology is similar to X 5, p. 292, 3 (τοὺς τῶν ἀγαθῶν δοτῆρες
θεούς, quoted above) describing the gods to which the theurgist
will be united. The similarity of expression adds further weight
to the argument that De Myst. X 5 and 6 describes Chaldaean rites.
The phrase Ζεὺς γάρ τοι δωτὴρ πάντων ἀγαθῶν τε κακῶν τε occurs
in Ch. Or. Fr. 215, 4.

[13]This illumination is discussed by Verbeke (379-380),
Lewy (198-199), and Nock (xcviii-c, esp. n. 6).

[14]The oracle at Clarus near Colophon is mentioned by
Tacitus, Annals 2.54. For bibliography on and further information
about this oracle, see M.P. Nilsson, Geschichte der Griechischen
Religion, 3rd edition (Munich 1967) I, 545-546, 545 n. 15, and II,
475 and n. 6.

[15]As Verbeke (380) notes.

[16]For the verb χωρεῖν as a "technical term," see des
Places (114), Nock (xcix n. 8), Lewy (40 n. 20), and des Places
in his edition of the Chaldaean Oracles, p. 152. The verb appears
in Ch. Or. Fr. 225 and describes the action of a δοχεύς. (See
note 7, above.)

[17]Iamblichus describes purification as one of the greatest
benefits from sacrifices (θυσίαι) in De Myst. V 6, p. 206, 16-17.
See also II 9, p. 87, 14-15, where Iamblichus says that "callers"
(οἱ καλοῦντες = κλήτορες) receive from the gods a release from
and transcendence over passions (παθῶν ἐξηλλαγμένην καὶ ὑπερέχουσαν); i.e., they are purified of them. For Iamblichus' doctrine
of the "caller" and its relation to Chaldaean elevation, see Lewy
(467-471).

[18]This fact is further confirmed by Iamblichus' use of
the word ἄνοδος (p. 41, 17) for the ritual--see Lewy (486 n. 6)--
and by the mention of συνθήματα ἀναγωγά (p. 42, 16). For
Chaldaean use of these "symbols" in the elevation, see Lewy (190-
192, esp. 192 n. 56). For the Iamblichean doctrine that the gods
do not descend into generation, see Julian, Or. IV.171B.

[19]On the word for "union," συναφή, see des Places (218),
who cites Nock (xcviii n. 5). Note that a similar distinction
between purification and divine union caused by illumination is

found in Iamblichus' accounts of the priestesses of Delphi and
Branchides (pp. 126, 4-127, 9).

[20]See Lewy (192-200).

[21]See Lewy (411 n. 37) for citations.

[22]A similar hierarchy is expressed in De Myst. II 5, p.
79, 6-13: "The power to purify souls is perfect (τέλεον) among
the gods and uplifting (ἀναγωγόν) among the archangels. Angels
free souls from the bonds of matter, and demons drag them down
into matter. Heroes lead them down to a concern for visible works,
etc." For the difference in the subtlety of light (λεπτότης τοῦ
φωτός) in gods and greater kinds, see II 8.

[23]In this part of the De Anima (pp. 454, 11-457, 6),
Iamblichus is discussing the judgment, punishment, and purification
of souls after death. However, since the purpose of the Chaldaean
elevation is the "soul;s immortalization" (Lewy [184 n. 32]), the
purification occurring as a part of the sacrament is the same as
that occurring after death. The initiate's soul becomes immortal
through elevation so that after death it can gain its reward.

[24]Note that at De An. I, pp. 455, 27-456, 1, the τέλος of
purification includes ἄνοδος ἐπὶ τὴν γεννησαμένην αἰτίαν.

[25]For the text, see Festugière (246 n. 2).

[26]Proclus, e.g., considered himself Mercurial; see Marinus,
Vit. Procl. 28, cited by Lewy (225 n. 197).

[27]A large part of this section of Proclus' commentary
(III, pp. 265, 22-266, 31), including the present passage, is
Iamblichean. This assertion is proved first by the citation of
Iamblichus' opinion concerning the vehicle at p. 266, 24-31
(= Iamblichus, In Tim. Fr. 84) and second by Proclus' two references
to the Chaldaean Oracles (p. 266, 18-23), which certainly derive
from Iamblichus' commentary on the Oracles. For evidence that the
view expressed in the present passage is itself Iamblichean, see
section III A, above. Festugière, in his edition of Proclus'
Timaeus commentary, V, p. 140 n. 4, compares In Tim. III, p. 268,
19ff. and 277, 8ff.

[28]And, for Iamblichus, this is a Chaldaean doctrine. For
the Chaldaean doctrine, see Lewy (211-213) and Ch. Or. Fr. 153
"Theurgists do not belong to the fated herd (εἱμαρτὴν ἀγέλην)."
Iamblichus has this oracle in mind in De Myst. V 18, p. 223,
9-15, where he states that "the great herd of humanity" (ἡ πολλὴ
μὲν ἀγέλη τῶν ἀνθρώπων) is involved with fate. See des Places
(172 n. 1). Iamblichus contrasts this great herd with the
theurgists, who escape fate (pp. 223, 15-224, 1).

[29]For Iamblichus as the source of Julian's writings, see Witt (35-63, esp. 36-39), Nock (lii), Lewy (69), and Wright (I, pp. 348-351, 441). Note Julian praises Iamblichus frequently: Or. IV.146A, 150D, 157D-158A; Or. VI.188B; Or. VII.217B, 222B, 235A; Ep. II and LVIII.401B. On the applicability of Macrobius to Iamblichus, see Witt (51): "Macrobius Saturnalia I.17-23 . . . [are] attributable to Iamblichus." Cf. Witt (38-39, 53) and Nock (lii n. 61; lv and n. 75; lviii and n. 88). For Julian and his relation to Iamblichean neoplatonism, see (in addition to Witt's article) R. Browning, The Emperor Julian (Berkeley 1976) p. 55; G.W. Bowersock, Julian the Apostate (London 1978) pp. 28-30, 86; and P. Athanassiadi-Fowden (Oxford 1981) pp. 143 and 153.

[30]The following summary of Chaldaean beliefs is from Lewy (137-157, 201-204). Cf. Athanassiadi-Fowden (note 29, above) 143 and n. 83.

[31]Cf. Wright (I, p. 357 n. 4) and Lewy (153 n. 317).

[32]On the Chaldaean conception of Aion as a fiery planet or sun, see Lewy (151-152).

[33]Cp. Dillon (343). Proclus follows Syrianus in placing the One above Aion, but even for Proclus Aion is a noetic entity. See Dodds (228), who cites Proclus, In Tim. III, p. 13, 22.

[34]See Dillon (29-33) for Iamblichus' elaborate ordering of the realm of the One. The realm consists of a completely transcendent One, a second more active One, a dyad of the limited and the unlimited, and finally the third One that Iamblichus equates with Aion.

[35]It should be noted that the Chaldaean Oracles themselves may not have been very clear about the identity of the third ruler. See the fragments cited by Lewy (142-144) and his reasons for identifying the third ruler with the moon. Since the moon was probably not specifically mentioned as the third ruler, it was easier for Iamblichus to interpret the Oracles as he did.

[36]In Iamblichean metaphysics, each hypostasis or realm consists of three moments: the unparticipated (ἀμέθεκτος), the participated (μετεχόμενος), and the relational (κατὰ μέθεξιν or ἐν σχέσει). The lowest moment of any realm is also the highest, unparticipated moment of the realm below it. Thus, for example, the Aion (or τὸ ἓν ὄν) is at once the lowest moment of the realm of the One and the highest moment of the noetic realm. On this aspect of Iamblichus' metaphysics, see Dillon (33-36, 52, 342).

[37]In Tim. Fr. 34. The translation is Dillon's (137). Dillon (418-419) also believes that Julian's Helios is the Demiurge.

[38]See also Sat. I.18.18: εἷς Ζεύς, εἷς 'Αίδης, εἷς Ἥλιος, εἷς Διόνυσος and compare Julian Or. IV.136A: εἷς Ζεύς,

εἰς Ἀΐδης, εἰς Ἥλιος ἐστι Σάραπις. On the relation between
these two oracular verses, see Festugière (159-160). Zeus is
another manifestation of Helios, as are Hades, Dionysus, and
Sarapis. As Festugière points out, Macrobius attributes his verse
to Orpheus and goes on to compare it to a verse from Apollo's
oracle at Clarus (Sat. I.18.20); Julian attributes his oracle
to Apollo (135D). The common source of both authors is Iamblichus.

[39]Cp. Macrobius, Sat. I.19.9: sol mundi mens est, where
sol = Ἥλιος and mens = νοῦς. The passage itself is cited by
Wright (I, p. 363 n. 3) as proof that Helios is νοῦς, and by
Lacombrade (202). The phrase is repeated in Macrobius, Sat.
I.18.17, where it is called Orphic. Cp. Sat. I.18.15.

[40]Cp. Proclus, In Tim. III, p. 82, 16-19, where the
Demiurge is said to create the sun from his own essence. The
sun is thus both hypercosmic and one of the seven planets (i.e.,
is encosmic). Proclus says this is a Chaldean belief. This
Proclean passage occurs in a longer one about the sun (pp. 81,
31-83, 17), which echoes much of what Julian says in his fourth
oration and can, therefore, be considered Iamblichean.

[41]The seven planets are (from highest to lowest in the
heavens) Saturn, Jupiter, Mars, the sun, Venus, Mercury, and
the moon. The visible sun is the spatial center as well as the
ruler. See Wright (I, p. 399 n. 3) and Lacombrade (111 n. 1).

[42]See Or. IV.156D-157A: "And now he [i.e., Helios],
shines into the visible realm, the center of all heaven, a seat
that is his from eternity, and grants a share of noetic beauty
to all the visible realm, and fills all heaven with as many gods
as he holds noerically in himself." Thus, Helios as the visible
sun occupies the center of the visible universe and creates from
himself the other planetary gods.

[43]It should also be noted here that Iamblichus believed
in the existence of gods above the noetic gods. These gods are
the so-called henads. See Dillon (412-416), who proves that
Iamblichus was the first to postulate the existence of henads.
Cf. Dodds (257-260) and the additional sources cited there. These
henads were horizontal emanations of the One and acted as the
first in a vertical series (σειραί) of gods. There is a manifestation of each henad at each metaphysical level. These henads
guarantee a connection from the realm of the One to that of
the visible gods--and below; for, the emanations proceed even into
the realm of generation. Julian notes that the emanations into
this realm are multiplied (Or. IV.142B, 143B). In this he
appears to be echoing Iamblichus (In Tim. Fr. 79), where Iamblichus
states that there is a doubling of the gods in their emanation
beneath the moon. For example, the 36 hypercosmic decadarchs
proceed as 72 sublunar gods. As Iamblichus notes, there is a
diminishing power along with the doubling in number. The series
of gods from the One to the sublunar realm guarantees a single

continuity throughout the universe, a continuity especially
helpful for the workings of theurgy.

[44]Cf. <u>Or</u>. IV.146D: the visible realm "is full of gods
from Helios" (θεῶν ἐστιν ἐξ Ἡλίου πλήρης).

[45]For Athene Pronoia, see <u>Or</u>. IV.149BC. Julian explicitly
compares Cybele and Athene with regard to their προνοητική at
Or. V.179B. Note that just as Cybele is "a virgin without a
mother" (παρθένος ἀμήτωρ, <u>Or</u>. V.166B), so too is Athene (<u>Or</u>.
VII.230A: τὴν ἀμήτορα, τὴν παρθένον; <u>Against the Galilaeans</u>,
235C: παρθένος ἀμήτωρ). Cf. Rochefort (112 n. 2).

[46]Julian refers to Helios as "the third demiurge" (165A,
161D). See Wright (I, p. 451 n. 3) and Rochefort (107 n. 2),
both of whom cite <u>Or</u>. IV.140A.

[47]This halt is symbolized by his castration (<u>Or</u>. V.167D,
169C).

[48]Thus Wright (I, pp. 451 n. 3 and 481 n. 2), Rochefort
(107 n. 2), Witt (51 n. 2), and Athanassiadi-Fowden (note 29,
above) 145 are wrong when they say that Julian "identifies"
Attis with the rays. There is a similarity, not an identity.
At <u>Or</u>. V.161D-162A, the critical passage, Julian says that Attis
is "the final nature of the third creator [i.e., Helios], which
descends by an excess of creative power through the stars above
down to earth." This statement does not imply that Attis is
Helios' rays but simply that Attis is the immanent creative power
of Helios carried in his rays.

[49]On the identity of τὸν ἑπτάκτινα θεόν with Helios, see
Wright (I, p. 483 n. 1) and Rochefort (183 n. 3).

[50]Strictly speaking, Attis descends only as far as the
Milky Way (<u>Or</u>. V.171A), i.e., as far as the moon (167D-168A).
However, Attis is the leader of the greater kinds (168AB: ἔξαρχον
δὲ τῶν θείων γενῶν, and cf. 168B, where Attis is flanked by
Corybants, αἱ τρεῖς ἀρχικαὶ τῶν μετὰ θεοὺς κρεισσόνων γενῶν
ὑποστάσεις). Thus, through them, he is connected to the sublunar
realm. Cp. <u>Or</u>. IV.145C, 151C.

[51]The purification is both physical and spiritual (<u>Or</u>.
V.178BC). For physical purification in Iamblichus, see <u>De Myst</u>.
V 16.

[52]See <u>De An</u>. I, p. 457, 13-14: The ancients assigned to
the soul παραπλησίαν τοῖς θεοῖς κατὰ νοῦν διάθεσιν ἀγαθοειδῆ.
See section I, above.

[53]See Lewy (183 n. 27), who, in addition, claims Iamblichus
as Julian's source.

[54] Julian does not say that Helios' ray is identical to the vehicle. This point is blurred by Rochefort (130), Witt (42-43, 46), and Lewy (183 n. 27). The ray and vehicle are similar because both are ethereal. Note that Iamblichus calls the vehicle αὐγοειδὲς πνεῦμα at De Myst. III 11, p. 125, 5-6 and V 26, p. 239, 9 and αὐγοειδὲς ὄχημα at III 14, p. 132, 12. See des Places (113 n. 1, 117 n. 3, and 182 n. 1).

[55] See Or. V.172BC: "This light [i.e., of Helios] has been shown to be related (οἰκεῖον) to the gods and to those [souls] eager to be elevated (ἀναχθῆναι)."

[56] See Or. IV.136B: ἀνατείνων τὰς ψυχὰς ἐπὶ τὸν νοητὸν κόσμον.

[57] See Kissling (320-321) and Dodds (316). See also the Introduction, above.

[58] See, for example, De An. I, p. 369, 12-15 and Festugière (194).

[59] See also De Myst. X 2, p. 287, 1-2: "No image is aroused when the noeric life is operating perfectly."

[60] It is by this means that divination occurs. See De Myst. III 11, pp. 125, 9-126, 3 and III 14, pp. 132, 18-133, 8.

[61] Cp. De Myst. III 7, p. 114, 7-8: in enthusiasm "the human διάνοια is not moved."

[62] Modern editors read the following: ψυχῆς κυβερνήτῃ μόνῳ θεατῇ νῷ. Iamblichus reads θεατῇ and omits νῷ altogether. See Dillon (253).

[63] A quotation from Phdr. 247c3. For Iamblichus, it is the noetic realm.

[64] See In Parm. Fr. 2A and Dillon (389-391). For the "flower of the intellect" as a Chaldaean term, see Ch. Or. Frr. 1 and 130, cf. 34, 37, 42, and 49. The ἄνθος τοῦ νοῦ "is the faculty which permits us to attain union (ἕνωσις) with the One," as des Places notes in his edition of the Chaldaean Oracles, p. 66. See also Lewy (165-169).

[65] The translation is Dillon's (201).

[66] The Demiurge is the most common goal given in the De Mysteriis. See, e.g., V 18, p. 223, 15-17: "A few who use a certain supernatural power of νοῦς separate from nature and are led around (περιάγονται) to a separate and unmixed νοῦς;" X 6, p. 292, 15-17: the goal of elevation (ἀναγωγή) for the Egyptians is the placement of the soul in the Demiurge; and X 7, p. 293, 12-13: ἐπὶ δὲ τὴν νοητὴν καὶ θείαν ἀναχθέντες.

[67]See Dillon (376), quoted in full in section II, above.

[68]Porphyry had argued that during the soul's descent, the soul gathered (in the words of Ch. Or. Fr. 61e) "a portion of ether, of the sun, of the moon, and as many things as float in the air." Although little evidence remains of Iamblichus' interpretation of this fragment, there is reason to believe that he thought that the ether, sun, moon, and air were not components of the vehicle but, rather, sources of ethereal light useful in theurgy. In De Myst. III 14, p. 134, 9-19, Iamblichus discusses divine illumination via heavenly rays (τῆς αὐγῆς ἔλλαμψις, line 11). This illumination holds as its greatest property a sacred radiating light (φῶς . . . ἱερὸν καταυγάζον, lines 14-15) "that shines down from above from the ether, or air, or moon, or sun, or any other heavenly sphere" (lines 15-17). Iamblichus, it seems, used this and other Chaldaean Oracles to show that all of the visible gods provided the divine light necessary for theurgic ritual.

[69]Plotinus is mentioned at 457, 6.

[70]Cp. ἄχραντον (380, 9), ἀπόλυτος (380, 12), and--with Festugière (244 n. 2)--συνοπαδοί . . . τῶν θεῶν (380, 24).

[71]See Lewy (213-226).

[72]According to Phdr. 246b6-7: "Every soul has a concern for everything without soul, and it revolves around all the heaven" (ψυχὴ πᾶσα παντὸς ἐπιμελεῖται τοῦ ἀψύχου, πάντα δὲ οὐρανὸν περιπολεῖ). Cp. De An. I, p. 458, 16-17: "According to the Platonists, souls have a concern for things without soul" (ἐπιμελοῦνται τῶν ἀψύχων).

[73]Cp. Sallustius XXI: souls "separated from their irrational nature and purified of all body are united to the gods and with them govern (συνδιοικοῦσιν) the whole cosmos." See also Nock (xciv n. 223).

[74]According to Phdr. 248e3-249b1, all souls except those thrice choosing a philosophic life return to this realm every thousand years. After ten thousand years, the whole cycle begins anew.

[75]Cp. De An. I, p. 458, 3-8, where Iamblichus contrasts the views of Numenius and the ancients concerning the souls union with the gods. Numenius conceives of such a union as "undifferentiated identity" (ταὐτότης ἀδιάκριτος); the ancients as a "conjunction with a different substance" (σύμφυσις καθ' ἑτέραν οὐσίαν). For Iamblichus, the soul, when it unites with higher entities, always remains a separate, inferior entity.

[76]In De Myst. X 5, p. 290, 10-14, Iamblichus makes clear that, at least in an earlier existence, the rational soul existed

164

alone, united to the gods, and only at a later time entered into combination with the irrational soul. Cp. VIII 6, p. 269, 1-12 and the notes of des Places (199, 222).

CONCLUSION

In the course of this study, it has been seen that Iamblichus
continually works on two levels: metaphysical and religious. With
regard to metaphysical philosophy, Iamblichus tries to reconcile the
works of Plato and to develop a consistent metaphysical hierarchy
based on the Platonic writings. With regard to religious and theurgic
beliefs, Iamblichus systematized the Chaldaean Oracles and reconciled
those divine pronouncements with the words of the divine Plato. Indeed,
Iamblichus' syncretism goes beyond this, as Iamblichus embraces and
reinterprets the Chaldaean, Hermetic, and Orphic writings and even
considers the Hermetic texts as the source for the philosophies of
Pythagoras and Plato.[1]

In trying to determine the origins of and the motivations
behind Iamblichus' religious/philosophical system, there is nothing
to be gained by claiming the superiority of either religion or
philosophy over the other. Both were necessary props for Iamblichus'
metaphysical system, and each reinforced the other. Theurgy was, of
course, superior to philosophy, but there was no choosing between
Plato and the Chaldaeans. Indeed, there is no conflict between them.
Iamblichus enfolds them both into a complete mutually compatible
system.

The metaphysical system that has been expounded in the
previous chapters shows Iamblichus working through the supposed
inconsistencies in the works of Plato himself: why does the human
soul fall, how does the Phaedrus myth with its chariot imagery
coincide with the Timaeus myth and its distributions and sowings of
the soul, can there be a final escape from generation? For Iamblichus,

165

there had to be one consistent answer.

But Iamblichus supplemented the Platonic texts with his own belief in theurgy. In order for theurgy to work, the metaphysical hierarchy of Plato must bear the additional burden of allowing the possibility of the soul's elevation. To his trained mind, all of Plato's works (which were themselves internally consistent) blended in perfect harmony with the ancient teachings of the theurgic priests.

In the end, Iamblichean philosophy can be said to consist in the harmonizing of the philosophies of past great thinkers. His philosophy can be summed up in his own words at De An. I, p. 366, 5-10. Although he is here discussing the human soul's inferiority to all the entities above it, the sentiment Iamblichus expresses is quintessentially his own:[2]

> These opinions are perfectly shared by Plato himself,
> Pythagoras, Aristotle, and all the ancients, whose great
> names are celebrated for wisdom, as one sees if one
> investigates their opinions with understanding
> (μετ' ἐπιστήμης).

The investigation μετ' ἐπιστήμης is the cornerstone of Iamblichean philosophy. Iamblichus is, certainly, a scholastic, but his own investigations allowed him not only to seek the answers in established texts but also to interpose his own ideas onto those texts (although, of course, Iamblichus would not see it this way).

This attitude of correct interpretation μετ' ἐπιστήμης is seen throughout Iamblichus' works but especially in the De Anima, which can be seen as a prolonged argument for the proper fusion of Platonic ideas with those of the theurgic priests. It can also be seen in the De Mysteriis, a blow by blow attack on Porphyry's Letter to Anebo, in which Porphyry assailed theurgy. Iamblichus

patiently rebuts Porphyry's every point and illustrates the truth:
theurgy is the human soul's link to the gods and the effectiveness
of theurgy is guaranteed by the metaphysical order in the universe.

Iamblichus' theory of the vehicle is also an investigation
μετ' ἐπιστήμης and an interpretation based upon the importance and
function of theurgic ritual and on the metaphysical hierarchy that
Iamblichus considered Platonic. According to Platonic and Chaldaean
doctrines (as interpreted by Iamblichus), the vehicle has three
functions. First, it houses the rational and irrational souls during
the descent to, sojourn in, and ascent from the realm of generation.
Iamblichus, drawing upon Plato's Timaeus, argues that the vehicle is
made from ether by the Demiurge himself. As such, the vehicle is
immortal. In its descent, the vehicle accumulates various powers,
lives, and bodies from the universe (i.e., from the gods, greater
kinds, and matter itself). In the soul's life on earth, the vehicle
can become associated with generation and weighed down by matter.
This material pollution keeps the soul from its appropriate rational
life. Thus begins the human's life of sin, the necessary judgment,
punishment, and purification after death, and the continual rebirth
in another human body.

The vehicle's second function is its capacity to transfer
sense impressions and other images to the soul. In this way, a mortal
can function in the world of the senses, perceiving this world,
remembering the past, and imagining whatever he likes. However, the
need for such images can help to hold the soul captive in this lower
realm.

The vehicle's third function is involved with theurgic

elevation. If a mortal can rise above the material realm while he is still living in it and can cast his eyes toward the gods, he can escape from the body and be united to the gods. The soul's ascent from this realm is brought about by the theurgic sacrament of elevation. In this theurgic act, the vehicle is purified from all material stains, its imaginative function is taken over by the gods, and it ascends via the divine ethereal rays to the circulation of its leader-god.

The concept of a soul's leader-god is, for Iamblichus, a Platonic one, drawn from his reconciliation of the Phaedrus and Timaeus myths. Each of the visible gods together with a complete retinue of greater kinds follows the Demiurge around the heavens and remains in contact with the Forms and gods in the noetic realm and with the One itself. The elevated human soul, its vehicle attached to its god's vehicle and its soul attached to the god's soul, can follow in this retinue and can also be united to the higher entities.

In this divine union, the rational soul is once again capable of the separate existence appropriate to it. The separated rational soul can climb upward to the One itself. After such a person's death his soul ascends immediately without judgment or punishment to the heavenly circulation and remains there until it is time for its next necessary descent, which it will accomplish purely.

In this way, Iamblichus conceives the role of the soul's ethereal vehicle. It remains forever the purified means of descent and ascent of the soul and plays a most important role in the theurgic ritual.

It has long been noted that the neoplatonic followers of

Iamblichus did little more than carry his philosophy to its logical
conclusion.[3] As has been seen, Syrianus and Proclus accepted

Iamblichus' metaphysical hierarchy and his emphasis on theurgy

almost without question. The same can be said for Iamblichus' theory

of the vehicle. Syrianus and Proclus accept the Iamblichean tenets

that the vehicle is ethereal, is created by the Demiurge, and is

immortal (Proclus, In Tim. III, pp. 235, 11-236, 6; El. Th. prop.

207 and 208). However, since they refuse to accept an immortal

irrational soul, they posit a second, mortal vehicle to house the

mortal, irrational soul (In Tim. III, pp. 236, 31-238, 26). Never-

theless, this second, mortal vehicle is composed of the four elements,

which are attached to the first vehicle in the soul's descent and

removed in its reascent.[4] This second vehicle is, therefore, akin

to Iamblichus' material envelopes that (he says) the vehicle gathers

in its descent.[5] Finally, Syrianus and Proclus accept both Iamblichus'

reconciliation of the Phaedrus and Timaeus myths and his conception

of the soul's leader-god.[6] Thus, although some changes were made

by later neoplatonists such as Syrianus and Proclus, these changes

were minor and concerned only small issues in Iamblichus' larger

conception. Iamblichus' theory of the role of the vehicle of the

soul continued almost unaltered in the philosophies of the later

neoplatonists.[7]

Notes to Conclusion

[1]See De Myst. I 1, p. 2, 2-3, where Iamblichus calls the
Egyptian writings Hermetic. At p. 4, 11-13, Iamblichus says he will
draw upon Chaldaean and Hermetic writings. At I 2, pp. 5, 14-6,
4, Iamblichus states that Plato and Pythagoras followed Hermetic
texts in their philosophies. See des Places' notes (38-41, 217)
and Scott (44-49). For Iamblichus as "an authority" on Orphism,
see Dillon (363).

[2]See also Julian, Or. IV.162CD, where the emperor, echoing
the teachings of Iamblichus, argues that the works of Aristotle
must be supplemented by those of Plato and that both of these must
be harmonized with the oracles of the gods.

[3]See, e.g., Wallis (142) and A.C. Lloyd, "The Later
Neoplatonists," in The Cambridge History of Later Greek and Medieval
Philosophy (Cambridge 1967) 302.

[4]See Festugière's notes in his edition of Proclus' Timaeus
commentary, pp. 102-103. There he refers to Dodds (320 and 302).

[5]See section I, above. For the difference between Iamblichus'
and Proclus' teachings about the irrational soul, see section III A,
above.

[6]In addition to the passages cited in section III A, above,
see El. Th. prop. 204 and 205.

[7]The later neoplatonists take Iamblichus' theory via Proclus,
and thus deny immortality to the irrational soul. Damascius accepts
Proclus' theory of two vehicles (the luminous vehicle is immortal,
the pneumatic vehicle that houses the irrational soul is capable of
a longer existence than the human body but is ultimately dispersed):
In Phaedonem I.168, 239, and 543; II.146. (Note that at I.168,
Damascius accepts the Iamblichean doctrine of theurgy's superiority
to philosophy.) See also Damascius' theory that the earth itself
has a luminous (αὐγοειδές), a pneumatic, and a visible body: II.141,
cf. I.508 and II.115. For the vehicle's imaginative faculty, see
II.38. Most significantly, Damascius seems to have rejected Proclus'
claim that the rational soul cannot exist separately from its vehicle
and to have accepted instead Iamblichus' theory that it can exist
separated in the hypercosmic realm: αἱ δὲ καθαρθεῖσθαι τελέως εἰς
τὸν ὑπερκόσμιον τόπον ἀποκαθιστάναι ἄνευ σωμάτων, I.551, and cp.
Iamblichus, De Myst. III 3, p. 106, 4. Cf. Westerink's note in his
edition of Damascius' commentary, ad loc. The neoplatonic school
at Alexandria also seems to have followed Proclus' revision of
Iamblichus' theory of the vehicle: for Ammonius, see John Philoponus'
commentary on Aristotle's De Anima 12.17-21, cited in Westerink's
edition of Olympiodorus' Phaedo commentary, p. 71. For Olympiodorus,
see In Phaedonem 3.4.8 and 13.3.10-12, along with Westerink's notes,
ad loc. For John Philoponus, see Kissling (322 and 324).

List of Works Cited

(i) Ancient Works

Aristotle. De Generatione Animalium. Ed. by H.J.D. Lulofs.
    Oxford: 1965.

Damascius. Dubitationes et Solutiones de Primis Principiis.
    Ed. by C.A. Ruelle. 2 vols. Paris: 1889.

----------. In Phaedonem, vol. II of The Greek Commentaries on
    Plato's Phaedo. Ed. with translation and notes by
    L.G. Westerink. Amsterdam: 1973.

Iamblichus. De Anima apud Stobaeus, Florilegium, q.v.

----------. De Communi Mathematica Scientia. Ed. by N. Festa.
    Leipzig: 1891.

----------. De Mysteriis. Ed. by C. Parthey. Berlin: 1857.

----------. Les Mystères d'Egypte. Ed. with introduction,
    translation, and notes by E. des Places. Paris: 1966.

----------. In Platonis Dialogos Commentariorum Fragmenta.
    Ed. with introduction, translation, and commentary by
    J.M. Dillon. Leiden: 1973.

----------. Protrepticus. Ed. by H. Pistelli. Leipzig: 1888.

Julian. Oeuvres Completès. Ed. with translation and notes by
    Bidez-Cumont-Rochefort-Lacombrade. 3 vols. Paris:
    1932-1964.

----------. Works. Ed. with introduction and translation by
    W.C. Wright. 3 vols. Cambridge: Harvard University Press,
    1913-1923.

Macrobius. Saturnalia. Ed. by J. Willis. Leipzig: 1970.

Olympiodorus. In Phaedonem, vol. I of The Greek Commentaries on
    Plato's Phaedo. Ed. with translation and notes by
    L.G. Westerink. Amsterdam: 1973.

Oracles Chaldaiques. Ed. with notes and translation by E. des Places.
    Paris: 1971.

Plato. Opera. Ed. by J. Burnet. 5 vols. Oxford: 1900-1907.

Plotinus. Enneads. Ed. with translation by A.H. Armstrong.
    3 vols. Cambridge: Harvard University Press, 1966.

171

172

----------. Opera. Ed. by P. Henry and H. Schwyzer. 2 vols.
Oxford: 1964 and 1977.

Porphyry. Sententiae ad Intelligibilia Ducentes. Ed. by
E. Lamberz. Leipzig: 1975.

Proclus. Commentarius in Platonis Parmenidem. Ed. by V. Cousin.
2nd ed. Paris: 1864.

----------. The Elements of Theology. Ed. with introduction,
translation, and commentary by E.R. Dodds. 2nd ed.
Oxford: 1963.

----------. In Platonis Rempublicam Commentaria. Ed. by G. Kroll
2 vols. Leipzig: 1899-1901.

----------. In Platonis Timaeum Commentaria. Ed. by E. Diehl.
3 vols. Leipzig: 1903-1906.

----------. Commentaire sur le Timée. Ed. with translation
and notes by A.J. Festugière. 5 vols. Paris: 1966-1968.

Sallustius. Concerning the Gods and the Universe. Ed. with
prolegomena and translation by A.D. Nock. 1926; rpt.
Cambridge: 1966.

Stobaeus. Florilegium. Ed. by C. Wachsmuth and O. Hense.
5 vols. Berlin: 1884-1923.

(ii) Modern Works

Armstrong, A.H. (ed.). The Cambridge History of Later Greek and
Early Medieval Philosophy. Cambridge: 1967.

Athanassiadi-Fowden, P. Julian and Hellenism: An Intellectual
Biography. Oxford: 1981.

Bidez, J. Vie de Porphyre. 1913; rpt. Hildesheim: 1964.

Bowersock, G.W. Julian the Apostate. London: 1976.

Browning, R. The Emperor Julian. Berkeley: 1976.

Burnet, J. Greek Philosophy: Thales to Plato. 1914; rpt.
London: 1932.

Cornford, F.M. Plato's Cosmology: The Timaeus of Plato Translated
with a running Commentary. London: 1937.

Dillon, J.M. The Middle Platonists. Ithaca: 1977.

Dodds, E.R. The Greeks and the Irrational. Berkeley: 1951.

----------. Pagan and Christian in an Age of Anxiety. Cambridge: 1965.

Festugière, A.J. La Révélation D'Hermès Trismégiste, vol. III: Les Doctrines de L'Ame. Paris: 1953.

Guthrie, W.K.C. A History of Greek Philosophy. V. Cambridge: 1978.

Kissling, R.C. "The ὄχημα-πνεῦμα of the Neo-Platonists and the De Insomniis of Synesius of Cyrene." AJP 43 (1922), 318-330.

Larsen, B.D. Jamblique de Chalcis. 2 vols. Aarhus: 1972.

Lewy, H. Chaldaean Oracles and Theurgy: Mysticism, Magic, and Platonism in the Later Roman Empire. Ed. M. Tardieu. Paris: 1978.

Morrow, G.R. "Necessity and Persuasion in Plato's Timaeus." Philosophical Review 59 (1950), 147-163.

Nilsson, M.P. Geschichte der Griechischen Religion. 2 vols. 3rd ed. Vol. 5, Part 2 of Handbuch der Altertumswissenschaft. Munich: 1967.

Rich, A.N.M. "Body and Soul in the Philosophy of Plotinus." Journal of the History of Philosophy 1 (1963), 1-15.

Rist, J.M. Plotinus: The Road to Reality. Cambridge: 1967.

Scott, W. Hermetica. Vol. IV. Oxford: 1936.

Smith, A. Porphyry's Place in the Neoplatonic Tradition. The Hague: 1974.

Taylor, A.E. A Commentary on Plato's Timaeus. Oxford: 1928.

----------. Plato: The Man and His Work. 6th ed. 1949; rpt. New York: 1963.

Tripolitis, A. The Doctrine of the Soul in the Thought of Plotinus and Origen. Libra Press: 1978.

Verbeke, G. L'Évolution de la Doctrine du Pneuma du Stoïcisme à S. Augustin. Paris: 1945.

Wallis, R.T. Neoplatonism. New York: 1972.

Witt, R.E. "Iamblichus as Forerunner of Julian." De Jamblique à Proclus. Ed. O. Reverdin. Geneva: 1975. 35-64.

Lightning Source UK Ltd.
Milton Keynes UK
UKHW041205230621
386021UK00001B/154